THE VIOLET BLOOD OF THE AMETHYST

LOUIS CALAFERTE

THE VIOLET BLOOD
OF THE AMETHYST

Louis Calaferte

Translated and Introduced by John Taylor

Chelsea Editions

Chelsea Editions, a press of Chelsea Associates, Inc., a not-for-profit corporation under section 501 (c) (3) of the United States Internal Revenue Code, has the support of the Sonia Raiziss Giop Charitable Foundation.

Le Sang violet de l'améthyste, Paris: Éditions Gallimard, 1998.

French text © 1998 Éditions Gallimard.
Translation, Notes, and Introduction © 2013 John Taylor.

All rights reserved. No part of this book may be used or reproduced in any manner whatsoever without written permission except in the case of brief quotations embodied in critical articles and reviews.

Author Photograph: Jacques Sassier, © Éditions Gallimard. Used with permission.

Illustrations, cover and page 21: Pages from the original manuscript, Bibliothèque Muncipale de Lyon. Used with permission.

Book design: Lisa Cicchetti.

Library of Congress Cataloging-in-Publication Data

Louis Calaferte, 1928–1994
The Violet Blood of the Amethyst
Translated and Introduced by John Taylor, p. 224

ISBN 978-0-9884787-4-9
1. Calaferte, Louis—Translation into English
2. Taylor, John, 1952–   II. Title

Manufactured in the United States of America by Thomson-Shore, Inc.

First Edition 2013

Chelsea Editions
Box 125, Cooper Station
New York, NY 10276-0125

www.chelseaeditionsbooks.org

ACKNOWLEDGMENTS

The translator would like to thank Daniel Lawless of *Plume* and Blandine Longre and Paul Stubbs of *The Black Herald* for publishing several sample poems and prose texts selected from this book. Many thanks also to Valérie Brantôme, who published samples on her literary website *Enjambées fauves*.

The Introduction was published by Peter Robertson, in an abridged version, in the *International Literary Quarterly* (April 2012). An abridged French version of the Introduction was given, as a paper, at the first Calaferte colloquium held in Blaisy-Bas on 5 November 2011. Let me thank Djamel Meskache, the director of the Éditions Tarabuste, for this opportunity. The text was subsequently published in the brochure *Louis Calaferte: Un lieu, une mémoire*, Saint-Benoît-du-Sault: Éditions Tarabuste, 2012.

The translator would also like to express his gratitude to the Sonia Raiziss Charitable Foundation, which awarded him a grant, in 2011, enabling him to find the time and energy to translate this remarkable book.

CONTENTS

Introduction   9

Le Sang violet de l'améthyste / The Violet Blood of the Amethyst   22

Notes   203

Bibliography   215

INTRODUCTION

When a friend who has never read Louis Calaferte (1928–1994) stands before a bookcase housing over a hundred volumes by this French writer, poet, playwright, and diarist, he or she inevitably asks: where to begin? It is easy to suggest Calaferte's moving first book, *Requiem des innocents* (1952), his erotic novel *Septentrion* (1963), or his short narratives depicting female sexuality, *La Mécanique des femmes* (1992); and, as complements, perhaps his memoir of the Second World War in Lyon, *C'est la Guerre* (1993), or the exposition of his Christian anarchist philosophy, *L'Homme vivant* (1994). Depending on the friend, some of Calaferte's plays, collected in six volumes at the Éditions Hesse, might be more suitable. Or his poetry, but Calaferte's prolificacy can be intimidating in this genre as well: the Éditions Tarabuste alone has issued over thirty titles.

As for myself, whenever I have taken on this informal advisory role, I have recommended *Le Sang violet de l'améthyste* ever since it appeared posthumously at Gallimard in 1998. First of all, *The Violet Blood of the Amethyst* enables one to break the critical habit of returning to the same handful of books; and notably the first one, *Requiem des innocents*, little matter how engaging and timely this memoir of growing up in an impoverished quarter of Lyon remains. Too often, critics (and well-meaning enthusiasts) mechanically cite this title, retell the story of the encouragement that Calaferte received from the writer Joseph Kessel, and then almost forget what has been written ever since then and awaits them on their desks. The same applies to *Septentrion*, the graphic eroticism and bold anarchistic underpinnings of which caused it to be legally restricted—in one of the rare cases of censorship in postwar France—to a "not for commercial sale" status for twenty-one years (1963–1984). The long-banned book thus has its own diversionary story to tell, and it should be told, but it can also divert attention away from what is essential: the contents of the book and its exceptional style. Of course, the two novels fully deserve their critical reputations, and especially *Septentrion*, which deepened Calaferte's approach and marked a new departure for him. But this is not my topic here.

The near-exclusive emphasis that is placed on them overlooks the glaring bibliographical fact that Calaferte, as far as prose is concerned, soon became essentially an author of *short* prose. Early books like *Satori* (1968) and *Rosa Mystica* (1968) already reveal the propensity to brevity and narrative fragmentation that informs nearly all his subsequent writing. Instead of expanding or amplifying, as a novelist or even a short story writer must do, Calaferte increasingly strives for formal compression, aphoristic acuteness, vivacity, tightness in a syntax that sometimes becomes less linked to that of colloquial speech, as well as—in apparent contrast—multifarious characters, narrative viewpoints, emotions, ideas, scenes, settings, and styles. Similarly, his poems are not only often short but also diversified in form, tonality, and contents. After the first decade of his literary career (during which he also publishes the novel *Partage des vivants* in 1953), his prose enters into broad generic categories like "poetic prose" or simply "short prose." (By the way, this latter novel, long out of print, has recently been reissued by the Éditions Tarabuste; and its narrative structure, sometimes built out of scenes not always connected to each other by smooth transitions, reveals that the author's sensibility was already oriented towards short prose.) He abandons the novel and ignores more traditional forms of the short story, two rare counterexamples of which constitute his book *Campagnes* (1979), which in turn is called a *récit* (narrative), in the singular. Indeed, he often produces books to which no conventional labels—novel, short-story collection, and even the rather vague and thus useful term *récit*—can be applied. If one wishes to grasp the whole writer, one must incorporate much more into the picture; and this much more is multifaceted, ever-moving, and often consists of what one might call "brevities" linked to other "brevities." These brevities are organized in such ways that the book, or the sequence of texts, delves, and from several angles, into its subject matter.

Hence the special significance of *The Violet Blood of the Amethyst*. The book displays the gamut of Calaferte's styles and themes, as well as several facets of his literary sensibility. There are poems (in various forms), short prose narratives (also in various forms), "notes" rather like some of those that fill his sixteen published *Carnets* (Notebooks), aphorisms, single sharp images removed from any explanatory context, and quotations ranging from verse by Emily Dickinson (whom he translates for the occasion) to a description found in Jean-Baptiste La Curne de Sainte-Palaye's *Mémoire de l'ancienne Chevalerie considérée comme un établissement politique et militaire*. The latter represents one of several similar discoveries made among the old editions that this very modern author also loved.

Calaferte juxtaposes erotic depictions with alchemical concepts, philosophical speculations, *seemingly* personal memories, a few observed or imagined childhood scenes and—most unexpectedly—laconic monologues spoken by Polyphemus, the Homeric Cyclops. The settings otherwise shift, though not uniquely, between two metaphorically antipodal cities, London and Venice, which respectively represent northern Europe—think of *Septentrion* once again—and southern Europe. The reader *believes* that the author is or has been in "ornate" Venice and "cottony" London, but this *autobiographical effect* may well be deceptive. Such is the case elsewhere, notably in the short prose texts that employ a narrative "I" in *L'Incarnation* (1987), *Promenade dans un parc* (1987), or *Memento mori* (1988).

And Time, too, is a central mystery in *The Violet Blood of the Amethyst*, a book in which countless questions are raised. Several historical periods are called up, and they thus extend—though in no linear order—from archaic Greece (with its resonant archetypal myths), through the Middle Ages, to the narrator's present, which is our present. Yet taken as a whole, the texts also seem to form the "present" of dreaming or, even more convincingly, of insomnia: those moments, minutes, or hours that parade by with their chaotic (and chronologically non-linear) images, memories, stories, aspirations, and thoughts, before the final two sentences can be spoken or heard: "Fear nothing. Fall asleep."

Other stylistic techniques or thematic ingredients that enter into *The Violet Blood of the Amethyst* have been used before by Calaferte, yet differently: for example, in the poetry collection *Londonniennes* (1985), the cruel narratives of *Portrait de l'enfant* (1969), the dialogues in Calaferte's plays (and in some of his prose works, even going as far back as *Requiem des innocents* and *Partage des vivants*), not to mention the erotic vignettes of *The Way It Works with Women* (the English title of *La Mécanique des femmes*). In this sense, *The Violet Blood of the Amethyst* is a sort of distillate; or a collection of distillates, depending on one's appraisal of the unity, or disunity, of the book. Implicitly asserting its coherence, Calaferte himself specifies in his fifteenth notebook, *Dimensions* (2009), which covers the year 1993, that *The Violet Blood of the Amethyst* also constitutes a "landmark," "marker," or "indicator." The writer refers (on December 23rd) to this book (and *Les Fontaines silencieuses*) as "book-bearings [*livres repères*] that are also poetic books [and] stand in a sort of zone parallel to the public." He also emphasizes their "high sincerity," which is a manner of stating their personal importance to him and the authenticity of his intent, though not, strictly speaking, any precise autobiographical inspiration. With respect to this latter critical question, time and again the reader must meditate on the first sentence of the book: "I call world that which does not resemble me."

Calaferte's initial efforts to write *The Violet Blood of the Amethyst* go back to 1989, five years before his death. In the thirteenth notebook, *Situation* (2007), which covers the year 1991, he mentions (on September 23rd) that the first pages had been written two years beforehand and then laid aside; and he observes that they have a "dreamlike vein," a remark hinting at the possibility that the sequence mirrors dreaming or insomnia. On the same day, he records his wife Guillemette's insightful reaction to these pages: "a fantastical and kaleidoscopic vision of our wounded and furiously eroticized world"—a statement putting the accent on what is outside, exterior: the world. This constitutes one of the essential dichotomies of the book. However, Calaferte adds that, for the time being, only the "entrancing" or "spellbinding" nature of the project entices him. Four days later, he abandons the manuscript once again in order to concentrate on *The Way It Works with Women*. Ultimately, *The Violet Blood of the Amethyst* will be mostly written after that book and before *C'est la guerre* and at about the same time as the posthumously published volumes *Maître Faust* (2001) and *Les Fontaines silencieuses* (2005).

Calaferte would work swiftly and intensely once inspiration had grasped him. His *Notebooks* recount sometimes rather long fallow periods, followed by prolonged bursts of exceptional creative energy. Several times in his *Notebooks* he writes of the importance, for a writer, of patience, of knowing how to "wait." The composition of *The Violet Blood of the Amethyst* is no exception. As his fourteenth notebook, *Direction* (2008), reveals, he was pondering the project again by February 26th (1992). A little less than three weeks later, on March 15th, he recommences work on its "fine mosaic." Typically, by March 19th, he has already produced fifty pages; and by March 29th he sees the end: "Begun on March 15th, *The Violet Blood of the Amethyst* is finished today. I need to put it in order, which is a fastidious task. I would like this odd book to have the perfection of jewelry work."

"Finished" thus means that the creative inspiration has run its course. There is still much work to be done which, presumably, engages the analytical intellect more than it does the other mental, emotional, and artistic qualities that have fuelled the composition of the individual pieces. This goal of ordering the texts seems to have been attained by June 26th, as a remark about the "mise au net" of the book and *Maître Faust* suggests. Two months later finds him continuing to translate poems by Emily Dickinson, the main tutelary figure of *The Violet Blood of the Amethyst*, which also reproduces lines by Martial, Propertius, William Blake, and others. In his labors to bring Dickinson into French, Calaferte chooses fifty-five poems from her work because of their "at once mystical and esoteric resonance." He hopes to "penetrate the magic, religious, and esoteric meaning of [Dickinson's] fascinatingly complex oeuvre." This same challenge faces the reader of *The Violet Blood of the Amethyst*.

Calaferte's own phrases—"fine mosaic," "jewelry work"—define this challenge on the structural level. To what extent is the book intricately arranged? Is it a mosaic, an artistic form that demands more attentive ordering and precise craftsmanship than a collage, let alone a simple collection of texts? A mosaic forms a pattern. Is there a "pattern" visible in *The Violet Blood of the Amethyst*? Back in 1991, when the author rereads the pages drafted in 1989, he notes (in *Situation*) that the initial construction of the book is "completely arbitrary" and that this "alarms" him.

At the minimum, *The Violet Blood of the Amethyst* is a commonplace book. Historically, the genre goes back at least as far as the thirteenth-century Italian *zibaldone*. Such hodgepodges collect sayings, maxims, topics, arguments, opinions, truisms, sundry quotations, and even drawings. They gather a writer's findings, what has influenced him (or what he wishes will influence him), what has amused him, what seems instructive, and thus reflect as much the whims and intentions of his mind as his practical writing routines (and, possibly, his search for inspiration). The English word "commonplace" translates the Latin *locus communis* ("widely applicable argument or thesis"), which in turn renders the Greek *koinos topos*. The playwright Ben Jonson's *Timber: Or Discoveries* (1640), for instance, is a commonplace book that includes experimental drafts, mini-essays, maxims, reflections, and examples of other genres. And so is, more or less, Leopardi's *Zibaldone*, compiled by the Italian poet and thinker (1798–1837) between 1817 and 1832. (Calaferte never saw the first full French translation of this book, which appeared in 2003.) Quoted on two occasions in *The Violet Blood of the Amethyst*, Leopardi put together an enormous journal particularly focused on philosophical ideas. But the Italian poet's *Zibaldone* is no truly representative example of the genre in that a commonplace book might comprise introspective jottings, but it is essentially open to the world in that it gathers what the writer comes across, not what he himself produces in terms of personal writings. This is not the case for Leopardi's masterwork. And there is a sense of usefulness to a commonplace book: it can be consulted by the author or by others. *The Violet Blood of the Amethyst* fits this definition, but there is much more to it.

An examination of the original manuscript confirms this. Calaferte wrote the first drafts of the short texts in a big notebook that also includes the daily jottings of his journal (which would become the volume *Direction*) and parts of a second book, *Maître Faust*. The texts in this original manuscript were typed up, then cut up and rearranged. The order in which they appear in the notebook differs greatly from that of the original French edition of *The Violet Blood of the Amethyst*. In addition, the manuscript reveals that the author originally intended to call the texts "Les Fontaines silencieuses." In other words, Calaferte inverted the titles of the two books.

The second epigraph gives the crucial hint as to why Calaferte rearranged the texts. "Unum in uno circulo sive vase" means "one thing in one circle or vessel." Already, a quest for unity is announced. Calaferte found the quotation in a footnote (about the hermetic *Tractatus aureus*) in Carl Gustav Jung's *Psychologie et alchimie* (French translation, 1970). The same Latin phrase is repeated in Jung's *Dreams*, to which Jung adds another footnote that provides the original context of the phrase: "The circumambulation has its parallel in the [. . .] 'circulation of spirits of circular distillation, that is, the outside to the inside, the inside to the outside, likewise the lower and the upper; and when they meet together in one circle, you could no longer recognize what was outside or inside, or lower or upper; but all would be *one thing in one circle or vessel* [my italics]. For this vessel is the true philosophical Pelican, and there is no other to be sought for in all the world.'"

This circularity, or unity, is difficult, if not impossible, to find because the world is full of disparities, conflicts, contradictions, oppositions. Calaferte hints that he has structured the texts of *The Violet Blood of the Amethyst* around this dilemma, not only by means of his second epigraph, but also when he refers almost offhandedly (and in parentheses) to "Apuleius's contradictory cross. *Alterutrae*." The key term "alterutrae" means "alternates," but it is used by Apuleius (in his logical treatise, *Peri Hermeneias*) in the sense of "contraries," "opposites," "contradictions." Apuleius was also fascinated by oppositions and potential unity. Similarly, although Heraclitus is not mentioned in *The Violet Blood of the Amethyst*, Calaferte elsewhere cites the pre-Socratic philosopher's related ideas; for example, the fragment: "Opposition brings concord. Out of discord comes the fairest harmony." This is one of the deepest movements, or leitmotivs, in Calaferte's entire oeuvre.

When reading *The Violet Blood of the Amethyst*, it is stimulating to keep in mind such "contraries" and, even more so, alchemists' searches to efface or dissolve the dichotomies of "inside" / "outside" and "lower" / "upper." On the one hand, the book displays or reveals what is "outside," in the "world," as is suggested by the aforementioned first line: "I call 'world' that which does not resemble me." But equally forcible is the impression that the book brings out what is "inside" a mind, be this mind the creative author's or—less autobiographically—a particular narrative "mind" that expresses not only some of its idiosyncrasies but also and especially representative elements of what Jung called "the collective unconscious"; that is, a mind employing a narrative "I" that would encompass more, as it were, than its strictly autobiographical circumscription; more than its "contents" based on personal experiences (of sundry mental and physical varieties); a mind that would be as much a receptacle as a fountainhead.

This narrative "I" in *The Violet Blood of the Amethyst* is compounded by the presence of other "I's." Sometimes even Polyphemus sounds like the poet: "I am the seer of all that remains unaccomplished." For this declaration expresses the thematic thrust of the book and resembles, in fact, the aforementioned characteristic movement or leitmotif in Calaferte's oeuvre: the elaboration of what is heading for some kind of "accomplishment" or ending; and this movement, moreover, seems to end with the previously mentioned solemn, soothing injunction: "Fear nothing. Fall asleep." An accomplishment that marks an ending or, rather—if one takes the author's hints—signifies that the alchemical circle has been formed once again, that the cycle has been renewed, that "accomplishment" implies continuity. Furthermore, Polyphemus tries to perceive who or what is stalking him, who or what will kill him. Does the Cyclops thus represent the author, who was writing this book as the signs of his fatal illness were becoming ever more pressing? This matters little. Polyphemus represents the fundamental condition of any human being: that of facing finitude, death.

The Violet Blood of the Amethyst is likewise permeated by the notion of a "return," a desire associated with Ulysses, who is Polyphemus's protagonist. The oft-evoked "sea" (*mer*)—with its tantalizing French homophone *mère* (mother) that is especially audible because of the conspicuous lack of definite and indefinite articles—is linked to this wish for a "return" and therefore to Ulysses the wanderer. Return implies circularity, once again, and recalls the archaic and mythological image of a snake biting its tail—the *ouroboros*, which is mentioned early on in *The Violet Blood of the Amethyst* and which is also the title of the bold "chant" written by Calaferte in an invented language in 1964, excerpted by Maurice Nadeau for *Les Lettres Nouvelles* in 1965, and reissued by the Éditions Tarabuste in 1995. This archaic image seems to materialize when the final sentence—about the narrator's falling off to sleep—rejoins the first sentence that announces the separation of the world and the narrative "I" (or the ego *tout court*) and thus acknowledges almost an awakening or a birth. *The Violet Blood of the Amethyst* likewise records halts and detours made during a journey—the journey of writing, of life (in its physical and spiritual aspects), an itinerary such as experienced Ulysses with all his multifaceted symbolism—aimed at gaining insight into an eternal cycle which promises to turn disparities and contraries back into sameness, oneness. Ulysses will be obliged to blind—essentially, to kill—Polyphemus. In *The Violet Blood of the Amethyst*, Polyphemus and Ulysses are essentially one and the same figure.

Similarly, *The Violet Blood of the Amethyst*—like other books by Calaferte—sets off what is "lower" against what is "upper," and points to or relates attempts to reconcile the two levels. Roughly stated, this vertical dichotomy involves a physical, natural, and/or sexual level and a mental and/or spiritual level. This spiritual or metaphysical level is nearly always present in Calaferte's writing, in one way or another. Here it is announced from the onset, in the first epigraph: "All then, in a word, who have spoken of divine things, both Barbarians and Greeks, have veiled the first principles of things, and delivered the truth in enigmas, and symbols, and allegories, and metaphors, and such like tropes." His use of *The Song of Songs* is also emblematic in this respect. Some passages state the dichotomy directly:

> Weight of the earth. Incommensurable mass. Laden with desire.
> Bodies are offered in their vulnerable opacity.
> Come—so that I may relieve you—so that together we may relieve ourselves.
> So that, through contradiction, we learn how to elevate ourselves.
> So that before returning to our mud, we rise through the levels of ether.

Analyses such as the preceding take Calaferte at his word in regard to epigraphs and key phrases found in the texts themselves. But are these exegeses going too far? Calaferte doubted that it was possible to analyze poetry. In *Choses dites* (1997), in regard to Verlaine's famous line "les sanglots longs des violons de l'automne" (literally, "the prolonged sobbing of autumn violins"), he maintains: "That is what poetry is. *It is nothing else* . . . You receive it. Without explanation." The title *Le Sang violet de l'améthyste* is "poetic" in this direct, immediate sense, not least in its surreal, oxymoronic, and mystical qualities; perhaps it essentially represented for Calaferte little more than a poetic *trouvaille*. The author's thoughts about the title are delineated nowhere in the *Notebooks*. This being said, the title itself expresses an extraordinarily rich dichotomy, even several dichotomies. The "violet blood" is contained in, flows through, the solid rock of the "amethyst," a gem which is fashioned from a fixed internal geometry and which, in Greek mythology and history, is symbolically associated with meditation, mental clarity, and peace of mind. The etymology of the word (Greek *a-methystos* "not drunk, not intoxicating") could not be clearer; the gem was thought to ward off both literal and metaphorical inebriation. "Blood" has its own spectrum of contrasting symbols, ranging from bodily passion and the blood of Christ to life. And one must never neglect the importance of this key-word, "Life," for the author of *L'Homme vivant*. In brief, the title forthwith suggests a struggle between Apollonian and Dionysian elements (to borrow Goethe's and Nietzsche's vocabulary), between an ideal serenity and life in its surging, inebriating, chaotic physicality. In *Passe-boules* (1995), this concrete poem expresses one side of the equation:

VIVRE
IVRE
à mourir!

The amethyst represents the other side. And this is why the title, *The Violet Blood of the Amethyst*, sums up Calaferte's entire oeuvre. Taken as a whole, Calaferte's oeuvre reveals a multifaceted literary sensibility, one aspect of which is pursuing truth not merely through poetry (and playful poetry), but also through logic, the precise alignment of words: syntax. This intellectual and stylistic intention is especially present in his aphoristic writings, in countless analytical passages of his *Notebooks*, as well as in some passages of *The Violet Blood of the Amethyst*.

The symbolic balance of the French title is thus crucial and argues for the decision to render it literally. The translation problem revolves around the color "violet." Generally speaking, when a French speaker perceives the color "violet," an English speaker perceives the same color as "purple." The adjective "pourpre" exists in French, even as "violet" exists in English, but when we say "purple," the French speaker will see and say "pourpre" if and only if there is a pronounced reddish hue to the purple;

otherwise, it will be "violet" in French. Moreover, descriptions of the gem "amethyst" in geology manuals give the color of the quartz as "violet" if the manual is French and most often as "purple" if the manual is English, even if (in English) a specific "amethyst violet" hue of purple exists and is described as being, once again, a reddish purple. Specifically, to cite *Webster's*, amethyst violet is "a variable color averaging a moderate purple that is redder and duller than heliotrope or manganese violet, bluer and duller than cobalt violet, and darker and slightly stronger than average lilac." A variable color, indeed!

Yet the arguments for rendering "violet" as "violet," and not as the somewhat more natural "purple," ultimately win out. The English "purple" as well as the thereby different French "pourpre" both connote imperial or regal rank, power, and wealth. Such considerations do not enter into Calaferte's symbolic matrix whatsoever, even negatively when he pays tribute to the impoverished poets Luís de Camões, Thomas Chatteron, and James Thomson. Calaferte describes the blood of the amethyst as being neither "pourpre," nor "rouge," nor "bleu" (which has still other connotations), but rather as "violet," which, as a "French" color, strikes a balance between blue and red. Less heavily laden with symbolism, violet is associated with Christian mystical unions of various kinds, with amorous fusion, as well as with submission—a theme present in some scenes—and melancholy. Qualifying blood with this adjective fashions a thought-provoking subtlety, a symbolic intricacy. Moreover, the word "violet" and its derivative "violine" appear only once each in the actual texts, yet "violent" recurs several times. A coincidence? It is hard to believe so when one reads Calaferte's remarks in his *Notebooks* about creating a "fine mosaic" and crafting "jewelry." Furthermore, Calaferte perhaps had a particular affinity with the letter "v," or attributed a special symbolic significance to it, as the countless fricative "v-sounds" in the invented language of his poem *Ouroboros* suggest. "Blood" appears often and variously. "Amethyst" shows up not even once, as if the gem were the form, the internal crystalline geometry, through which the texts—the violet and sometimes violent blood—were flowing, giving life to the form, to the book, constructing it. *Unum in uno circulo sive vase* . . . Ultimately, the alchemical phrase says all. *The Violet Blood of the Amethyst* seeks wholeness and gives it a form.

Translating Calaferte is no easy matter. Besides the difficulties of rendering a few quotations originally penned in older French and of finding equivalents for the French translations that the author uses for some Latin verse and that also sometimes possess archaic diction, his style itself exhibits idiosyncrasies. Most striking of all is the near-systematic suppression of articles at the beginning of many sentences and invocations, most conspicuously for the key word *mer*. This absence of definite and indefinite articles can suggest jotting down notes (as in a commonplace book), but beyond this stylistic habit, and because of it, physical matter surges forth in all its immediacy, substantiality and timelessness. I have nearly always mirrored Calaferte's French in such cases and have attempted to remain as close as possible to the word order, all the more so in that logic—the conflict of contraries and their potential resolution—and thus syntactic logic are at stake in the book. Although he is an author inclined to realistic, even clinical precision, Calaferte also employs various philosophical abstractions that call for careful scrutiny before finding English equivalents. And there are numerous recurrent key terms, some of which are abstract and others more concrete; reoccurrence itself is significant, as I have already suggested above in regard to the alchemical epigraph and especially the question of an inherent "pattern." Although a French word often has a broader semantic range than its English equivalent, even its cognate, I have respected these lexical and conceptual leitmotifs in most cases. The reader will want to pay attention to words (or their derivatives and synonyms) such as "approach," "return," "lace," "image," "decorate," "unfulfilled," "russet," "slender," "sleep," "shroud," "know" (or "misknow"), "innocent," "child," "name," "destiny," "relinquish", "form" (or "shape"), and "conform"—just to mention a few.

Such issues were discussed at length with Guillemette Calaferte, in letters and on the telephone. This translation has benefited from her many insights into both semantic and stylistic questions. In order to seek specific sources for quotations and to elucidate a few uncertain passages, she retrieved the original manuscript, which is included among the Calaferte Papers in the Municipal Library of Lyon. In the process, the French version offered here makes a few minor corrections to the original Gallimard edition. May my longtime friend be thanked *de tout coeur*.

Thanks to Guillemette Calaferte and her son, Guy Delorme, I was able to consult this manuscript at the Calaferte colloquium which was held in Blaisy-Bas on 5 November 2011 and at which I gave a paper, in French, drawing on this introduction. I would also like to acknowledge my friend, the writer and art critic Gilbert Lascault, who pointed out those "v-sounds" in *Ouroboros*. As with all my translations, my wife Françoise Daviet-Taylor was a perspicacious reader of the first drafts of this version.

Writing about Dickinson and implicitly about his project to translate her, Calaferte underscores in *Direction*, on September 23, 1992, the necessity of "bringing out her intelligence, her knowledge, the depth and gravity of her thinking, her singular temperament, her mysticism, her anguish before death." Communicating that necessity, while translating this emblematic book, has been my goal here.

John Taylor
Saint-Barthélemy d'Anjou
November 30, 2012

LE SANG VIOLET DE L'AMÉTHYSTE

THE VIOLET BLOOD OF THE AMETHYST

Ainsi l'on peut dire que tous ceux, Barbares et Grecs, qui ont traité de la divinité, ont occulté les principes des choses et ont transmis la vérité par des énigmes et des symboles, par des allégories et des métaphores et autres semblables figures.

— Saint Clément d'Alexandrie
(*Stromate* V – IV, 21, 4)

Unum in uno circulo sive vase.

All then, in a word, who have spoken of divine things, both Barbarians and Greeks, have veiled the first principles of things, and delivered the truth in enigmas, and symbols, and allegories, and metaphors, and such like tropes.

—Saint Clement of Alexandria
(*The Stromata* V – IV, 21, 4)

Unum in uno circulo sive vase.

J'appelle monde ce qui ne me ressemble pas.

M'approprier cet inappropriable de ton regard
où es-tu par les yeux ?
lointaine, sur l'ombre mouvante de la mer devant toi ?
attachée à des instants sans prolongements ?
vide de pensées, d'envies, immobile dans le non-conformé ?
ailleurs
dans des ébrindillements d'images qui ne te sont que bribes de souvenirs impossibles à reconstituer ?
dans ton vouloir durci ?
dans ce que ce regard se refuse à exprimer, à laisser approcher, à seulement laisser deviner ?
je suis proche de toi
nous marchons en parlant
tu me souris
ta langue m'embrasse
je caresse à deux mains la longueur de ton corps de jeune femme
je pourrais doucement relever tes tissus et te faire debout l'amour contre l'arbre qui nous semble proposé
je pourrais faire gémir ton ventre
peu à peu te dissocier de toi-même jusqu'à l'incontrôlable folie des arrachements
mais — ton regard ?

Dessin en V renversé du toit sur l'uniforme grisure du ciel. Une cheminée fume par régulières boules bleutées. Derrière la maison, treillis sombre du sommet de l'arbre. Des fils électriques croisent l'espace. Les murs de pierres sont froids dans leur impénétrable ancienneté. Quelque chose de léger remue au souffle du vent. La vie est cristallisée. Temps soudain devenu comme palpable. Vieillissement, rouille, fissures. Fleurs récemment écloses, herbe au vert sifflant, terre réchauffée.

J'attends mes demains de vie. Mes demains d'absence.

I call world that which does not resemble me.

Appropriate for myself that inappropriable quality of your gaze
where can you be found through your eyes?
remote, on the moving shadow of the sea in front of you?
attached to moments of no consequence?
empty of thoughts, cravings, and motionless in what has not been conformed?
elsewhere
among images twigged out into bits of memories impossible for you to piece back together?
in your hardened willpower?
in what this gaze refuses to express, to let be approached, even guessed at?
I am near you
we walk along and talk
you smile at me
your tongue kisses me
my caressing hands go up and down your young woman's body
I could softly lift each cloth and make love to you standing up against this tree that seems offered to us
I could make your abdomen groan
little by little dissociate you from yourself until the uncontrollable frenzy of wrenching apart
but—your gaze?

Inverted V of the roof against the uniform grayness of the sky. Same-sized bluish balls of smoke rise from a chimney. Behind the house, the dark trellis of the top part of the tree. Electric wires crisscross through the air. The stone walls are coldly, impenetrably ancient. Something light stirs whenever the wind blows. Life is crystallized. Time suddenly seems palpable. Ageing, rust, cracks. New blossoms, whistling green grass, warmed-up soil.

I am awaiting my tomorrows of life. My tomorrows of absence.

Serpentaire (rapace qui chasse les serpents dont il se nourrit)
Serpenteau (petit serpent, pièce d'artifice)
Serpentant (ce qui serpente)
Serpenter (avoir un cours sinueux)
Serpentin (tube en spirale servant à faire tenir une grande longueur de tube dans un récipient de dimensions limitées. Longue bande étroite de papier coloré enroulée sur elle-même)
Serpentine (silicate de magnésium hydraté)
Serpette (petite serpe)
Serpent (reptile sans membres, se déplaçant par reptation. Personne perfide et méchante. Instrument de musique à vent)
Serpent, rival de l'homme — trait vivant, *ouroboros*, abstraction sans fin.
Serpent, à la fois mâle et femelle — âme et sexe.

Mer — étonnante.
Scandale de t'approcher sans Femme.

Rideaux anciens de coton brodés de motifs géométriques ; entremêlement de losanges en bandes droites, avec un timide essai de fleurs au centre innocemment incrusté de chrismes.
Ce n'est là qu'ouvrage de patience
de mains adroites
de bon vouloir
d'occupation de jours.
Leur tulle masque la fenêtre, embellissant le lointain d'un flou à couleur de rêve.

— Qui es-tu, toi, l'homme à l'œil nu ?
Polyphème se détourne, chagriné.
— Je suis l'inégal, murmure-t-il, mon unique chance serait d'être commun. Quelle pitié !

Serpentaire (the serpent-eater, a bird of prey that hunts and feeds on snakes)

Serpenteau (a little snake, a serpent in fireworks displays)

Serpentant (snaking, winding, meandering)

Serpenter (to snake, to wind, to meander)

Serpentin (a coil, a spiral tube used for maintaining a long length of tube in a container of limited size; a streamer, a long thin spiraling band of colored paper)

Serpentine (serpentine, magnesium silicate hydroxide)

Serpette (a little billhook, a pruning knife)

Serpent (a limbless reptile that crawls. A snake, meaning a nasty and deceitful person. A bass horn)

Serpent, man's rival—a lively stroke of the pen, *ouroboros*, an endless abstraction.

Serpent, both male and female—soul and sex.

Sea—surprising.

Scandal of approaching you without Woman.

Old cotton curtains embroidered with geometric patterns; an intermingling of diamonds in narrow bands, with a timid attempt at depicting flowers in a middle naively encrusted with chi-rhos.

It's only a work of patience
done by skillful hands
by good will
a daily pastime.

Their tulle covers the window, embellishing what lies in the distance with a dream-colored blur.

—You there with your one naked eye, what man are you?

Polyphemus turns away in distress.

—I am the unequal one, he mutters. My only hope would be that this state were common. What a pity!

Fuite — qui est mon désir.

Dans le temps, sa forme même est devenue informe.

Désir qui n'est plus qu'appréhension d'une nostalgie, d'un vague qui ne se recompose pas seul.

Désir, qui fut un fait, une présence, un nom, une activité si fort souhaitée — pour n'être plus que dispersement.

Les choses ne meurent pas d'avoir été, mais de n'avoir pas été poursuivies.

Sans doute est-il nécessaire qu'après avoir été insaisissable, le désir soit déclin.

Ne reste que *l'ombre*.

À demi nue étendue sous la pelure du soleil dans une lascive attitude.

Se fait entendre à peu de distance le régulier ressac de la mer.

Sur toutes ses façades, la maison est grande ouverte à la chaleur.

Le luxe n'est plus qu'oubli.

Une suite d'imperceptibles additions.

Son adversaire est simple respiration de Femme soulevant lentement deux seins aux pointes dures.

La minceur d'un corps comme abandonné aux heureux accidents du temps.

La coquille d'un sexe refermé entre la puissance courbe des cuisses.

Le luxe est un ventre.

Plaisir prévu.

Écarte un peu tes lèvres, remue légèrement une jambe, ouvre-toi à peine, montre ta langue, plisse les yeux, pose tes mains sur tes seins, défais-toi de toi-même, pense à ces bouleversements secrets qui façonnèrent ton corps de Femme, prépare l'amour, sois nerfs, tête battante, soupirs, râles, affaissements, poursuite aiguë de l'exaltation renouvelée, sois lumière dans cette Italie vacante où seuls deviennent époux érotisme et mort.

Complique-toi, que chacune de tes parcelles soit difficile à ourdir, puis à transformer.

Demain, nous serons dans l'une des villes les plus froides du monde.

Escape—which is my desire.

With time, its very shape has lost its shape.

Desire that is no longer but apprehension of a kind of nostalgia, a moody vagueness unable to put itself back together on its own.

Desire that was a fact, a presence, a name, strongly wished-for acts—and that has ended up mere dispersion.

Things don't die because they have been, but because they haven't been kept going.

It likely follows that desire, after having been ungraspable, becomes decline.

Only *the shadow* remains.

Half-naked, stretched out beneath the peel of the sunlight in a lascivious position.

Nearby, the steady backwash of the tide can be heard.

On all sides, the house is wide open to the heat.

Luxury has become mere oblivion.

A succession of imperceptible sums.

Its adversary is simply Woman's breathing, her two breasts with their hardened nipples slowly rising.

The slenderness of a body seemingly given over to the fortuities of time.

The shell of a sex enclosed between the curved power of her thighs.

Luxury is an abdomen.

Planned pleasure.

Open your lips a little, slightly move a leg, barely open yourself up, show your tongue, squint, place your hands on your breasts, undo yourself from yourself, think of those secret upheavals that fashioned your Womanly body, prepare the lovemaking, become nerve endings, throbbing brain, sighs, groans, giving in, keenly seeking out the renewed exaltation, be bright light in this vacant Italy where only death and eroticism become husband and wife.

Become more complicated. May every bit of you be difficult to warp, then transform.

Tomorrow, we'll be in one of the coldest cities on earth.

Ce qui, depuis longtemps, parfois depuis des siècles, vient à moi dans le silence, l'ignorance réciproque, pour que je brise, mette un terme ; pour que je sois artisan d'une composition nouvelle de formes ; à ma façon démiurge, mais sans volonté prononcée ; facteur, peut-être, de vies recommencées, d'isolements, de rassemblements futurs ; cette incalculable longueur de chemin qui m'était réservée, depuis quelles origines ? — pour sûrement m'atteindre dans la naïve destination qu'un « autrui » espérait de moi, puisque seule, à l'instant précis, ma présence prenait valeur significative d'acte accompli — il y a eu mort, dissociation, éparpillement ; j'ai cassé l'objet qui, en les décorant, a accompagné tant de vies. J'ai cassé ce qui ne devait pas m'appartenir.

    Le mot n'est qu'envol.
    Poursuivre l'idée — qui s'exile.
    La reconnaître, la saisir, la posséder, la faire usure.
    Cet immobile du rien — dans l'abolition.

Avec une innocente simplicité, Phèdre constate que : *dans une humble condition les hommes n'ont rien à craindre, et que les grandes richesses sont accompagnées de périls.*
De quelle façon faut-il, en toute sécurité, porter son âme ?

    Dans le jardin de ma jeunesse
    dans les roses de mon jardin
    dans le visage de mes roses
    dans le sourire de mon visage
    dans la tristesse de mon sourire
    dans les sables de ma tristesse
    dans la solitude de mes sables
    dans la mort de ma solitude
    dans l'enfantillage de ma mort

What has been coming to me silently, without either of us knowing, for so long, sometimes for centuries, so that I may shatter, put an end to; so that I may become the craftsman of a new composition of forms; in my own way a demiurge, though with no expressed will to be one; perhaps the creator of lives begun again, of solitary withdrawals, of future gatherings; this immeasurably long path that was reserved for me, yet starting from what origins?—surely in order to join up with me in the naïve destination that an "other" hoped would be mine, since only my presence, at that precise moment, took on the significant value of an accomplished act—there was death, dissociation, scattering. I broke the object which, by decorating so many lives, accompanied them. I broke what was not supposed to belong to me.

    A word merely takes flight.
    Go after the idea—that goes into exile.
    Recognize it, grasp it, possess it, make use of it.
    This immobility of nothingness—in the abolition.

With innocent simplicity, Phaedrus acknowledges that *poverty is safe; great riches are liable to danger.*
How must one, in complete safety, bear one's soul?

    In the garden of my youth
    in the roses of my garden
    in the faces of my roses
    in the smile of my face
    in the sadness of my smile
    in the sands of my sadness
    in the solitude of my sands
    in the death of my solitude
    in the childishness of my death

Ce soir de lente promenade entre les grands arbustes — où tu pouvais aussi bien être l'enchanteresse que la mort.

Tu t'étais vêtue de velours noir qui t'étreignait le corps, et tu marchais pour moi, impatiente de me connaître, de me réduire à toi par toutes les sorcelleries de la séduction.

J'écoutais ta voix jeune, ton rire jeune, j'avançais à côté de ce corps jeune — mais je devais m'en aller le lendemain même pour cette capitale où m'attendait une autre femme, dont les pouvoirs étaient incomparables.

Je ne dis rien. Je songe.

Tout nous est rapprochement pour nous devenir lande aveuglée.

Lève les yeux devant toi : le soleil est rose.

Senteur puissante des herbes guérisseuses, dont le parfum est depuis toujours inexplicablement gravé dans ma mémoire.
Nous fûmes enfants d'Éden.

Elle désirait avoir chaud, être nue sur des chemins de plage à l'air concassé par le soleil d'après midi.

Ambition de créer des inexistants.

Grisâtrerie crépusculaire.
L'âme est entre Dieu et Diable.

Picotements de la branche de thym jetée à la flamme de la cheminée.
Essentiel de vie qui se consume.

That evening when we slowly strolled between the high bushes—when you could just as well have been the enchantress as death.

You were dressed in tight-fitting black velvet and, impatient to get to know me, to reduce me to yourself by all the witchcraft of seduction, you were ambling along just for me.

I was listening to your youthful voice, your youthful laughter, I was moving forward alongside that youthful body—but I was supposed to leave the very next day for that capital where another woman awaited me. Her powers were incomparable.

I say nothing. I daydream.

Everything brings us together and becomes our bedazzled heath.

Look straight ahead: the sun is rose-colored.

Strong scented healing herbs whose fragrances have ever, inexplicably, been etched in my memory.
We were children of Eden.

She wanted to feel hot, to walk naked on beach paths, the air crushed by the post-noon sun.

Ambition to create inexistent entities.

Twilight grayishness.
The soul between God and the Devil.

Tingling of the thyme branch tossed into the flames of the fireplace.
One of life's essentials is burning up.

Venise, la contournée.
Pluie. Mer grise. Femme altière. Femme devin.
Venise pleure. Venise larmoie.
Tu étais dans la nuit d'étoffe des chambres une beauté nue extraordinairement distincte. Silence, d'une épaisseur de fruit. Demain, tu appelleras les oiseaux.
Mer chantonnante. Port étroit.
Femme au nom des froideurs du Nord.
Venise, tourbillon épuisé.
Au café de l'élégante place dentelée, nous boirons un *caffellatte*. Tu caresseras ma main sur la table. Tes doigts, savants insectes.
Venise, la close.
Nous parlerons de nos poètes aimés, de nos peintres aimés, de nos musiciens aimés. Nous nous tairons. (Il y a une jeune servante au corps conçu pour les perditions amoureuses. Elle s'appelle Alma. Elle a l'extrême jeunesse des sciences anciennes.)
Toi, germination des abondances. Ton nom est le Nom.
Venise n'est que refus.

Je m'admets — je cherche.
Je me poursuis moi-même.

Polyphème, forgeron des feux de l'Etna.

Transgression est affirmation — affirmation, renouvellement.
Le libre se contient dans : *Je m'oppose*.
Puis, d'autres sommes de transgressions afin de s'opposer à cette opposition.
Une confection maille à maille — tissage de rudesse, sinon de violence.

Matinée pure de son regard.

Ornate Venice.

Rain. Gray sea. Haughty woman. Divine woman.

Venice is weeping. Venice is whimpering.

In the cloth-lined nights of bedrooms, you were an extraordinarily distinct naked beauty. The silence: thick like fruit. Tomorrow, you'll call out to the birds.

Sea humming. Narrow harbor.

Woman whose name is coldish like the North.

Venice, weary whirlpool.

At the café on the elegant lacey square, we'll drink a *caffellatte*. You'll caress my hand on the table. Your fingers: learned insects.

Venice, the closed city.

We'll speak of our beloved poets, beloved artists, beloved musicians. We'll become silent. (There's a young servant whose body has been conceived for amorous perdition. Her name is Alma. She has the extreme youthfulness of ancient sciences.)

You, germination of abundances. Your name is the Name.

Venice is nothing but rejection.

I accept myself—I seek.

I'm the one who pursues myself.

Polyphemus, blacksmith of the fires of Etna.

Transgression is affirmation—affirmation, renewal.

Freedom is contained in: *I am opposed.*

Then, other transgressions add up to oppose this opposition.

Stitch-by-stitch sewing—a rugged, if not violent, weave.

Pure morning of her gaze.

Brusque jetée bleue dans l'assombrissement des terres.
Ici,
quelque chose s'achève pour un inaccessible recommencement.
Espace étranglé par la fragile décoration des roseaux déployés.
Rouge et bleu, une barque frissonne sur l'eau,
comme partagée entre un désir d'évanouissement et celui de se confier à la terre, de s'y calfeutrer.
Barque et homme ne sont qu'un.
Mer — seule.

Voir l'innocence mourir.

Tu couches lentement sur mon ventre ta tête aux cheveux éclaboussés
mon sexe coule entre tes lèvres

J'insinue le doute dans l'orbe de ma réflexion.
Je me propose en rudiment explorateur.
Je me détourne des illusoires routes droites.
Je me défais pour me reconstituer.
Vérité du changement.

Dans l'immense jardin embaumé, chaque plante s'exerce à s'identifier.
Moi — et moi — et moi.
— Quel est ton nom ?
— Serpent. Et toi ?
— Malédiction.
L'Arbre dit :
— Je suis l'Intouchable.
Une hiérarchie, déjà, s'organise.
Adam dit :
— Je suis Homme.
Eva :
— Liberté.

Abrupt blue jetty in the darkening lands.
Here,
something comes to an end for an inaccessible renewal.
Expanse strangled by a fragile decoration of spread-out reeds.
Red and blue, a boat shivers on the water,
 as if hesitating between a wish to vanish and a desire to confide itself to the shore, to warm up there.
Boat and man are but one.
Sea—alone.

To see innocence die.

Slowly you put your head, your splattered hair, on my stomach,
my sex slides between your lips.

I make doubt creep into the orb of my thought.
I offer my services as an exploratory rudiment.
I turn away from illusory straight roads.
I undo myself in order to put myself back together.
Truth lies in change.

In the vast fragrant garden, every plant learns how to identify itself.
Me—and me—and me.
—What's your name?
—Snake. And you?
—Malediction.
The Tree says:
—I'm The Untouchable.
A hierarchy is already getting organized.
Adam says:
—I'm Man.
Eva:
—Freedom.

Viens jusqu'à moi — d'abord traversant la chambre secrète. La largeur de tes pas ne saurait s'inscrire dans la largeur des miens ; nous sommes rigueur et légèreté, lueur et obscurité, paume et revers de la main de science.

Puisqu'il est dit que nous devons renoncer à l'amitié, fais l'expérience du Feu — entre dans l'innomé.

Plissements d'eau dans la petite rivière dorée de soleil —
des dispersions vives de poissons qui ne sont, peut-être, qu'ombres d'eux-mêmes ; image de ce qu'ils proposent à l'enchantement puéril de l'œil.

Brusques cliquetis pétillants d'argenterie moussante, fugaces éclats d'émeraude enchevêtrés de saphir, de turquoise

fines coulances insituables

échappements

moulineries de vie

dans d'imprévisibles danses sinueuses.

J'étais là, un matin, seul, les pieds avancés dans l'eau, contemplant la brillance floue de ces amusements ingénus ; poissons de si petite taille que le grossissement de l'eau avantageait ; présent à leurs jeux brusquement éparpillés par on ne savait quelle frayeur ancestrale, envoûté par la joliesse, l'infinie capacité de liberté —

qui étais-je dans ma masse vulnérable ?

que m'était-il autorisé ?

ni vagabondages de rivière ni envols dans l'espace.

J'apprenais à être de la terre.

Main d'enfant.

Dame, ne vous desplaise se ceste dame ou damoiselle va devant ; car, combien qu'elle ne soit ni noble et si riche comme vous, elle n'est point blasmée, ains est mise au nombre des bonnes, et ains ne dit l'on pas de vous, dont il me desplaist ; mais l'en fera l'honneur à qui l'a desservi, et ne vous en merveillez pas.

Come over to me—first crossing the secret bedroom. The width of your footsteps can't fill out mine; we are rigor and lightness, gleam and obscurity, the palm and the back of science's hand.

Because we are fated to give up being friends, then experience Fire—enter what is nameless.

Water rippling on the sunlit stream—
vivid scatterings of fish that are perhaps mere shadows of themselves; images of what they offer to the eye's childish enchantment.

Sudden jingling, twinkling of foaming silverware, fleeting flashes of emerald entangled with sapphire, turquoise

fine lines vaguely flowing past

escapes

life milling

in unpredictable winding dances.

I was alone there one morning, my feet in the water, contemplating the blurry brilliance of those ingenuous amusements; tiny fish enhanced when magnified by the water; I was attentive to their games abruptly broken up by some strange ancestral fright, was bewitched by the grace, the infinite capacity of freedom—

who was I in my own vulnerable mass?

what was I allowed to do?

neither swim off into the stream nor fly off into outer space.

I was learning to be of this earth.

A child's hand.

My Lady, do not be displeased if this lady or maiden go before you; for, although she is neither as noble nor as rich as you are, she is blameless and is thus admitted to those who are good, and this is not said of you, who displease me; but will honor whomever has done a disservice to her, and do not marvel at this.

Mer — innombrable.
Je suis tes respirations, tes perpétuels essais de reformation.
Je suis mon regard perdu par ton éloignement.
Ta gaieté des matins lavés.
Ton ouverture à la masse d'infinis.
Étincelante, tu appartiens à l'arsenal de mes plongeons oniriques.
Mer — insatiable.

Exceptionnellement malheureux par le cœur.
La force dynamique de la vie m'emportait.
Les incertitudes de l'avenir.
Images de l'enfance à concrétiser.
Violences à exercer, comme pour se supplanter soi-même.
Sexe à contenter dans la rage et l'inconscience.
Recherche d'une assise, d'une stabilité, d'un axe, d'une confiance.
Me troubler, me renoncer pour devenir moi.
M'exiger, ne pas me convenir.
Écouler les années — devenir.

Rues mélancoliques et vides où nous étions conflit.

Les concordances sont de brèves collusions accidentelles d'une mosaïque en composition.

Non me définir, mais me dissimuler en vue d'une ressemblance qui aurait tes sonorités.
Devenir femme accomplie ; de la sorte être incorporé à la mesure de l'autre partie du monde.
Linge intime, robes, maquillage — la métamorphose effleure l'âme ; je te rejoins pour te mieux méconnaître.
Nous progressons péniblement dans le chaos des torsions du Sexe — que ce martyre t'échappe, quoi de plus naturel ?
Tu es fixité pour salaire de mon angoissante mouvance.

Sea—countless.
I follow your breathing, your perpetual attempts at reformation.
I follow my own gaze vanishing because you are afar.
Your cheerfulness of mornings washed clean.
Your openness to the mass of infinities.
Scintillating, you belong to the arsenal of my dreamy diving.
Sea—insatiable.

An exceptionally unhappy heart.
The dynamic force of life bore me off.
The uncertainties of the future.
Images of childhood to specify.
Violent acts to exert, as if to supplant oneself.
A sexual organ to satisfy rashly, with rage.
Searching for a base, stability, a direction, confidence.
Disturbing myself, giving up on myself, in order to become myself.
Demanding from myself, not suiting myself.
Clearing away the years—becoming.

Empty, melancholy streets where we were conflict.

Agreements are brief accidental collusions of a mosaic in composition.

Not define myself, but rather conceal myself with the prospect of a resemblance having your sonorities.

Become an accomplished woman; in that way, be incorporated on the same scale as the other part of the world.

Lingerie, dresses, makeup—the metamorphosis lightly touches the soul; I join you in order to better misknow you.

We struggle forward among the chaotic twists and turns of Sex—it's only natural that this martyrdom escapes you.

You are steadfastness for the wages of my anxiety-ridden mobility.

Je n'occupe pas la totalité de l'espace de mes possibles.

Il m'importe qu'autrui me soit signe métaphysique.

L'homme savait sur le monde trop de choses pour lui être soumis.
Sa science s'exerçait à la distance, autrement dit à la délivrance
à l'irrépressible expansion du libre
donc — à la SOLITUDE.

Qu'apprend-on ? Que la clarté est abstraction.
Je marche vers le vide d'un moi-même qui ne sait pas renoncer.

Dans cette belle chambre calme de Londres, où les nuits nous recevaient en passagers clandestins — drolatiquement vêtue d'une longue chemise à rayures rouges, pieds nus, tu étais l'indéfectible jeunesse.
Ta voix légère, point trop juste, chantant par bribes un poème de tu ne savais qui, évoquant les rues froides de la ville où, le soir, s'enlaçaient des amoureux.
Les démons de ton enfance étaient encore présents dans chacun de tes gestes, chacune de tes intonations.

Poudre argentée de la rose blanche.
Comme le regard, le parfum est langage.
Je donne à la fleur secrète le nom de mes évanescences les plus indisciplinées.
Elle est elle et moi.
Le lendemain matin — pétales éparpillés sur le sol.
Tant de choses intimes viennent de disparaître à jamais.

I do not occupy the whole space of my potential.

That another person is a metaphysical sign for me matters to me.

Man knew too many things about the world to be subjected by it.
His science learned what distance is, in other words deliverance
the irrepressible expansion of what is free
thus—SOLITUDE.

What do we learn? That clarity is abstraction.
I am heading toward the emptiness of a myself who does not know how to give up.

In that nice calm room in London, where nights welcomed us in as clandestine passengers—barefoot and drolly dressed in a long red-striped shirt, you were indestructible youthfulness.

Your lighthearted voice, not too perfectly in tune, singing bits of a poem whose author was unknown to you and which evoked the cold streets of the city where lovers hugged each other in the evening.

The demons of your childhood were still visible in each movement of your hands, in each of your intonations.

Silvery powder of the white rose.
Like gazing, fragrance is language.
I give to the secret flower the name of my most unruly kinds of evanescence.
The flower is itself and me.
The next morning—petals scattered on the ground.
So many intimate things have just vanished forever.

Nuit, confinement.
J'arpentais mes questionnements, mes projections, mes éventuels accomplissements.
Je me faisais rêve existant.
J'étais solitude de l'apprentissage.
Explore ta nuit indéfinie.

La petite fille dit :
— Quand j'étais plus petite, je croyais qu'apprendre était mal, que ça n'aboutissait qu'à se rendre supérieur aux autres pour s'en moquer.
Yeux de profondeur candide.

L'un vers l'autre.
Tension accentuée des attentes.
Le rapprochement n'est qu'angoisse décuplée.
Aveuglante, la seconde du revoir.

Lucain, le poète, se fait, pour mourir, ouvrir les veines par son médecin.
Tragique instant de la cassure où, moribond, le génie de l'homme se soucie encore des vers de sa composition qu'avec faiblesse il récite.
Celui dont Montaigne dit « qu'il le préfère volontiers, non tant pour son style que pour sa valeur propre et la vérité de ses opinions et jugements ».
Lucain, l'intrépide, le nouveau — nœud du poème :

> *Les ormes tombent ; l'yeuse s'ébranle sur son tronc noueux ; l'arbre de Dodone, et l'aune qu'on lance sur les flots, et le cyprès qui n'annonce pas une tombe plébéienne, perdant pour la première fois leur vaste chevelure, et, dépouillés de leur feuillage, laissent pénétrer le jour. Toute la forêt chancelle ; mais sa masse épaisse la soutient dans sa chute.*

Souple, l'équation ainsi se profile-t-elle : Lucain veut vivre sous la tyrannie de Néron.
Sous la tyrannie de Néron, les poètes meurent. À vingt-sept ans.

Night, confinement.

I would pace up and down over my questionings, my predictions, my potential accomplishments.

I would turn myself into an ongoing dream.

I was the solitude of apprenticeship.

Explore your infinite night.

The little girl says:

—When I was littler, I thought learning was bad and only ended up making you superior to others so you could make fun of them.

Deep candid eyes.

Each heading towards the other.

Tension accentuated by expectation.

Getting closer increases anxiety tenfold.

The dazzling second when they spot each other again.

When he wanted to die, the poet Lucan had his doctor open his veins for him.

The tragic moment of breaking off when the dying poet's mind still cares about his verse, which he feebly recites.

He whom Montaigne "likes best of all, not so much for his style as for his worth and the truth of his opinions and judgments."

Lucan the intrepid, the innovator—the crux of the poem:

> *Down fall the ash trees, the knotty holm-oak is hurled down; the wood of Dodona, too, and the alder more suited to the waves, the cypress, too, that bears witness to no plebian funeral mourning, then first lay aside their foliage, and, spoiled of leaves, admit the day, and thrown down with its trunks thickly set the falling wood supports itself.*

The flexible equation implies this: Lucan wants to live under Nero's tyranny.

Under Nero's tyranny, poets die. In their twenty-seventh year.

Polyphème se dit :

— Les dieux m'ont voulu à l'image de l'inévitable, de l'insurpassable Force, celle qui règne sur les espaces, qui est toute violence, toute obscurité, entêtement obtus. Ainsi, les dieux m'ont-ils voulu roi, riche de troupeaux, invincible dans ma stature, intouchable dans mon antre. Qui saurait dire que ma laideur épouvante sans dire d'abord ce que sont Beauté et Laideur ? Ce qui respire, palpite en moi, dans ce secret qui a nom Polyphème, lequel peut en avoir connaissance, en juger ? Quelque intuition funeste cependant me prépare au crime dont la perversion de la différence se fera un délice d'user contre moi afin de m'anéantir dans ce que je suis. Fils des mers et des profondeurs, ô Neptune, mon père, ô Thoosa, ma mère, pourquoi m'avoir enfanté si, dans la nature, je devais être accroc, violation de la règle ? Désiriez-vous mon malheur, ou n'étiez-vous qu'insouciance ? Tous me sont ennemis, danger ; mon sang avant le leur, mais l'angoisse qui m'oppresse a dans le monde un nom que, pour ma faiblesse, j'ignore, encore qu'il me sera un jour fatal. Ô dieux inégaux, que mes souffrances me soient supportables — épargnez-moi la nuit.

Regard grave de l'enfant puni pour un mensonge dont, à tort, on l'a accusé.
Quelque chose en lui se forme d'inconnu, qui, après l'incompréhension affolée, s'appellera haine.
Si peu que ce fût, sa vie désormais est ombrée par cet empêchement qu'en vain il s'efforce de s'énoncer à lui-même dans l'espoir de se retrouver tel qu'il se connaissait sans surprise avant l'incident ; il faudrait pour cette sorte de purification l'accompagnement d'il ne sait quelle tendresse.
Il est seul — homme.

À moi-même mystère.

Dans les rues du matin
sa joie sautillante, inaperçue des passants préoccupés.
Elle était l'éblouissement trouble de ce court fragment de liberté.

Poussière grise de la lumière de ce jour de pluie.

Polyphemus tells himself:

—The gods wanted me to be the very picture of the inevitable, unsurpassable Force that reigns over all expanses and that is wholly violent, wholly obscure, entirely obtuse. The gods thus wanted me to be a king with a wealth of herds, my stature invincible, untouchable in my cave. Who would claim that my ugliness terrifies, without first saying what Beauty and Ugliness are. Who can know, or judge, what breathes and palpitates in me, inside this secret that goes by the name of Polyphemus? A deathly intuition, however, prepares me for the crime that the perversion of difference will delight in turning against me in order to annihilate what I am. Son of the seas and the depths, O Neptune my father, O Thoosa my mother, why did you give birth to me if, in Nature, I was to be a breach in, a violation of the rule? Did you desire my misfortune or were you only heedless? Everyone is my enemy, danger; my blood before theirs, but the anxiety oppressing me has, in this world, a name I don't know even if it will one day prove fatal to me—and this is my weakness. O unequal gods, may my suffering be bearable—spare me night.

Grave look in the eyes of the child punished for a lie of which he has been falsely accused.

After the panic-stricken incomprehension, something unknown takes shape in him and will be called hate.

As minor a matter as this was, his life henceforth lies in the shadow of this impediment that he vainly attempts to formulate to himself in the hope of becoming once again he whom he knew himself to be, before the surprise of the incident; this sort of purification would need to be accompanied by a kind of tenderness that he cannot define.

He is alone—a man.

A mystery to myself.

In the morning streets
her bouncy joy, unnoticed by preoccupied passersby.
She was the suspicious dazzle of this short sequence of freedom.

Gray powdery light of this rainy day.

Le feu végète dans la cheminée.
La maison est un peu froide.
Il se pourrait que, dans ce cocon paralysé, nul d'entre nous n'existât réellement ; jamais n'eût existé.
En de tels jours d'enrobement narcotique, peut-être notre sensibilité est-elle conviée à imaginer celui des morts ?
C'est dimanche.

Venise — pétrifiée
fille du délaissement.
Elle était enfouie sous le duvet laiteux des fourrures, un immobile sourire dans les yeux.
Ruelles griffonnées où nous marchions seuls.
— Je me sens plus hautaine que la ville.
Premiers flocons d'une petite neige.

Qu'est-ce que comprendre ?
S'inverser.

Margelle de la nuit.

Avec ton clair visage, tes caressantes lèvres, ton pur regard, tes gestes gais de *menteuse*.

Mouvement sur le sol à peine perceptible, d'une apitoyante, émouvante lenteur ; maladresse dans une direction qui s'ignore, soudain se contrarie, se reprend, se reperd, s'obstine à se perdre, à se reprendre — sur le sol hostile, mouvement qui est imitation, parodie, essai ivre, toutefois persistant.
Infinitésimal signe de vie — qui lutte, obéit à sa pensée, à son vouloir, tente d'obtenir — quoi ? de *vivre*.
Un brusque déplacement, et c'est la mort.
Notre mort — qui est ce déplacement.

The fire barely burns in the fireplace.
The house is a little cold.
In this paralyzed cocoon, perhaps none of us really existed; never existed.
On such narcotic-coated days, is our sensibility perhaps summoned to imagine the day of the dead?
It's Sunday.

Venice—petrified
daughter of neglect.
She was buried beneath the milky down of furs, a motionless smile in her eyes.
Scribble-like alleyways where we walked alone.
—I feel haughtier than this town.
First flakes of a little snowfall.

What is understanding?
Inverting oneself.

Edge of the well that is night.

With your luminous face, your caressing lips, the pure look in your eyes, your cheerful gestures of a *liar*.

Along the ground, a barely perceptible movement that is pitifully, touchingly slow; awkwardly heading in an unknown direction, then suddenly thwarted, correcting itself, losing its way again, stubbornly losing its way, correcting itself once again—on this hostile ground, movement that imitates, parodies, reels like a drunk, nonetheless persists.
An infinitesimal sign of life—struggling, obeying its mind, its will, attempting—what exactly? *To live.*
One abrupt move, and it's dead.
Our death—which is that move.

Main habile
　　main aux doigts de féerique façonnière
　　main d'une femme de Cos
　　qui mêla d'or la pesanteur des tissus dont la jeune Némésis ornait son corps
　　　　se laissant dans sa beauté admirer par les rues de la ville
　　　　froide de vengeance
　　　　généreuse de haine
　　　　indifférente
　　　　étrangère au pardon
　　　　comme un don d'elle-même
　　　　refermée dans la pénible impossibilité d'assouvir les désirs sur son passage suscités
　　　　ardente et glaciale.

　　Midi — enfant aux lèvres écarlates.

　　J'ignore qui tu es devenue, mais ma pensée ne saurait vivre sans toi, ni mon corps, que tu habites de tes perversions douces.

　　Je devine que tu es rétive à l'offrande de quelque chose de toi qui ne soit pas que ton corps.
　　Je te hais.
　　Tu n'obtiendras rien de moi.
　　Tu es ma licence.
　　Ma première musique de mort.

　　Italie grise —
　　des exubérances factices
　　des profondes consciences du délestement
　　des retirements infranchissables
　　des pauvretés souriantes et criminelles
　　Italie des départs.

Deft hand
hand with its skillful fairylike fingers
hand of a woman of Kos
who mixed gold into the weighty fabrics embellishing the body of young Nemesis
who in turn let her beauty be admired by the streets of the town
Nemesis cold with vengeance
generous in hate
indifferent
a stranger to forgiveness
as a gift of herself
shut up inside the painful impossibility of assuaging the desires provoked by her passage
a woman ardent and icy.

Noon—scarlet-lipped child.

I have no idea whom you have become, but my mind wouldn't know how to live without you, nor my body, in which you dwell with your sweet perversions.

I surmise you're rebellious to the idea of offering something of yourself that is more than your body.
I hate you.
You'll obtain nothing from me.
You're my licentiousness.
My first death music.

Gray Italy—
of artificial exuberances
of deeply conscious self-renunciations
of impossible self-withdrawals
of smiling, criminal poverties
Italy of departures.

Je m'approchais pour la savoir présente.
Les rues de Londres avaient un léger goût de poussière.

Dans les grands lits frais que nous réserve le hasard du voyage, nous sommes instants de caresses éruptives
    ta main rampante sait trouver et prendre
    jusqu'au plaisir aigu
    que ta langue recueille.

Bach — la déchirure.

Pureté rare de la lumière crépusculaire, à la fois onctueuse, laiteuse, transparente, au reflet bleuté.

Nos alliances sont mathématiques.

La gaie science.

Je me présente, lucide, dans la figuration qui est à mes yeux mienne — je ne sais que penser ni dire. Qui ai-je présentement devant moi ? Ces cheveux épars dressés autour de ma tête comme une auréole blanche, ce visage usé, creusé, mais qui exprime sa continuité de force. Ai-je au cours de ces années vécues engrangé suffisamment pour me modifier ? Certes — mais mon ambition dernière est d'être l'innocence de l'enfant ; s'il se peut, celle du nouveau-né, du Souffle de la Création. Je veux être un mort jeune.

J'entrouvre tes cuisses et regarde fixement cette échancrure — bouche avide du monde.

I was coming closer because I knew she was present.
The streets of London had a slightly dusty taste.

In the big fresh beds that the vicissitudes of the journey keep in store for us, we are moments of eruptive caresses
    your groping hand knows how to find and grasp
    all the way to the acute pleasure
    that your tongue gathers.

Bach—the heartbreak.

Rare pureness of the dusk light, at once creamy, milky, transparent, with bluish reflections.

Our alliances are mathematical.

The merry science.

Clearheaded, I come forward in the role I believe is mine—not knowing what to think or say. Who is this standing in front of me now? These scattered hairs standing on end around my head like a white halo, this worn, hollow-cheeked face nonetheless expressing its constant force. During my lifetime, have I garnered enough to modify myself? Surely—but my last ambition is to attain a child's innocence; if possible, a newborn baby's innocence, the Breath of Creation. I want to be a young deadman.

I half-open your thighs and stare at that plunging cut—a mouth eager for the world.

Sous le pontificat d'Alexandre VI, le minéralogiste Michele Mercati et son ami, le philosophe Marsile Ficin, s'entretiennent des possibles directions de l'âme après la mort ; se promettant mutuellement que le premier des deux qui disparaîtra fera en sorte, avec l'aide de Dieu, d'avertir l'autre sur ce qu'il en est de la vie éternelle.

Quelques jours après cette conversation, Mercati entend de bonne heure le matin un cheval passer à toute bride devant sa fenêtre, qu'il ouvre, stupéfait, apercevant, monté sur un cheval blanc, un fantôme qui lui crie au passage : *Vera, vera illa sunt !* fournissant ainsi à son ami confirmation de la réalité d'une seconde vie.

Mercati n'apprend que plus tard que Marsile Ficin avait rendu l'âme à la minute même où il l'avait vu galoper sur le cheval.

Comprends ce que je ne puis dire.

Le rideau est d'un rouge ombré, d'une lourdeur ondulante ; principe de dissimulation dans des chambres trompeuses. Les hautes fenêtres ouvrent sur des balcons qui surplombent des rues de feux nocturnes. Dans cette proximité de l'obscur, sois silhouette illusoirement présente. (Son rouge à lèvres est d'une profondeur opaque, d'une épaisseur ondulante ; principe de dissimulation dans des expressions tortueuses.)

Polyphème s'endort :

— Je sais que je suis Personne, mais que Personne n'est pas un nom digne qu'on y accorde attention.

La réflexion le tire de sa somnolence.

— Quels sont ces mots qui viennent me hanter le cerveau, alors que je n'en connais pas même le sens ?

Il s'enfonce plus profondément sous la peau de bête qui le recouvre pour la nuit. Il a peur.

— Polyphème a peur, constate-t-il avec quelque honte et, incompréhensiblement, une espèce d'étrange soulagement.

Son œil se clôt.

— Que suis-je en train de devenir ? Que seront les miens lorsque les temps se seront succédé ?

Under the pontificate of Alexander VI, the mineralogist Michele Mercati and his friend, the philosopher Marsile Ficin, discuss the possible directions the soul might take after death. They promise each other that the first one to die will, with the help of God, inform the other one about eternal life.

A few days after this conversation, Mercati hears—early one morning—a horse galloping past his window. Opening it, he is startled to see a phantom riding a white horse and shouting out while going by: *Vera, vera illa sunt!* This thus confirms for his friend the reality of a second life.

Mercati learns only later that Marsile Ficin gave up his soul at the very minute he was seen galloping by on the horse.

Understand what I cannot say.

The heavy, wavy, shadowy red curtain; the concealment principle in misleading rooms. The tall windows open onto balconies looking down on streets with nightly traffic lights. Be a deceptively present silhouette in this close darkness. (Her lipstick is deeply opaque, wavy, thick; the concealment principle in tortuous expressions.)

Polyphemus drowses off:
—I know I am Nobody, but Nobody is a name unworthy of interest.
The thought draws him out of his sleepiness.
—What are these words that have come to haunt my mind when I don't even know their meaning?
He snuggles more deeply beneath the animal hide covering him for the night. He is afraid.
—Polyphemus is afraid, he admits with some shame and, incomprehensibly, a strange sense of relief.
His eye closes.
—What am I becoming? What will my kin and kind be like when eras have come and gone?

Brusquement, il pousse un rugissement qui ébranle la grotte jusque dans ses recoins lointains.

— Je sais encore rugir ! Je me reconnais ! se dit-il, rassuré.

Ce grand café pour nous devenu lieu rituel
où
malgré la présence des autres consommateurs
tu avais l'amoureuse habilité des caresses obscènes
folle de nous
de Sexe
pressée d'aller ensuite dans les jardins proches
y être Femme suprêmement démoniaque
le monde autour de nous aboli
éteint
par la force noire de ton insurpassable désir de chair.
Tu devenais CORPS — le langage même se métamorphosait.

Nous étions à l'âge de l'heureuse confusion de l'enfance, qui ignore le désastre de la mort.

Londres — voix sourde.

Je marche à ton pas, accroché à ta main étroite ; l'étoffe se froisse sur tes cuisses ; tu es murmure évaporé.

Nous cherchions une librairie de livres anciens ; les noms des grands écrivains anglais de jadis qui, avant nous, flânèrent ici caracolaient dans ma mémoire ; hier, ou le jour d'avant, je t'avais fait vivre de Shelley et de Coleridge ; nous nous étions noyés dans la vague inquiétante, la fulgurance retenue d'Emily Dickinson.

I heard a Fly buzz — when I died

Nous avions bu le vin noir de William Blake, l'alchimiste.

Earth rais'd up her head
From the darkness dread and drear

Suddenly he roars, making the furthest recesses of the cave shake.
—I still know how to roar! I haven't lost my powers! he tells himself, reassured.

That big café became a ritualistic meeting place for us
where
despite the presence of other customers
your loving skill applied its obscene caresses
you were crazy about us
about Sex
in a hurry to proceed to the nearby gardens
where you would be a supremely demoniacal Woman
the world around us abolished
extinguished
by the dark force of your unsurpassable lust for flesh.
You would become BODY—language itself would metamorphose.

We were at the age of the cheerful confusions of childhood and unaware of the disaster of death.

London—muted voice.
I walk in step, holding your thin hand; the cloth creases between your legs; you are an evaporated murmur.
We were looking for a bookshop selling old editions; the names of the great English writers from times past who strolled here before our time were prancing about in my memory; yesterday, or the day before, I had nourished you on Shelley and Coleridge; we had drowned ourselves in the disturbing groundswells, in the restrained intensity, of Emily Dickinson.

>   *I heard a Fly buzz—when I died*

We drank the black wine of William Blake, the alchemist.

>   *Earth rais'd up her head*
>   *From the darkness dread and drear*

Londres — gant feutré.

Vouloir hostile — qui *cache*.

Jardins de poivre.

Toi — insolence.

Je t'ai regardée beaucoup aujourd'hui, dans l'attendrissante faiblesse de ce qui, un jour, sera ta beauté de Femme ; songeant au roi Nebucadnetsar, qui fit faire une statue haute de soixante coudées, large de six, qu'il dressa dans la vallée de Dura, province de Babylone.
C'est sous l'enveloppe de douceur de ton sommeil que j'aimerais t'immortaliser.

Attentes
alarmes du désir
(qui seras-tu derrière la parure nouvellement inventée afin d'aiguillonner et ton plaisir et le mien ?)
Qui seras-tu que tu ne sois toujours ?
Je ne suis pas homme à me laisser prendre aux apparences — mais j'en accepte le jeu.
J'attends dans ma solitude consentie le faux-semblant de ton divertissement de jeune fille dévergondée.
Ce que tu ne peux par la puissance de tes fards et de tes déguisements, c'est t'évader de toi-même.
Je te souhaiterais *redevenue* — mais déjà est couverte une partie du chemin, qui t'a définitivement façonnée.
Où est cette enfance qui, peut-être, te recherche ?

J'étais ton spectateur-miroir.

London—felt-lined glove.

Hostile willpower—that *hides*.

Pepper gardens.

You—insolence.

I looked often at you today, at the touching weakness of what one day will be your Womanly beauty; and I was dreaming of King Nebuchadnezzar who had a statue sixty cubits high, six cubits wide, erected in the Valley of Dura, in the province of Babylon.
It's beneath the soft envelope of your sleep that I'd like to immortalize you.

Expectations
alarms of desire
(who will you be behind the finery newly fashioned in order to goad both your pleasure and mine?)
Who will you be that you've not always been?
I am not a man to be taken in by appearances—but I accept the game.
In my agreed-upon solitude, I await your loose girl's sham entertainment.
What you can't do with your potent make-up and disguises is to escape from yourself.
I wish you could *once again become* as you were—but part of the path that has definitively fashioned you has already been trodden.
Where is the childhood that is perhaps seeking you?

I was your mirror-spectator.

Au réveil — le vide, qui n'a plus même forme de toi. Mon angoisse, mon malaise te réclament, mais je suis sans voix.

Le sujet s'invente — ne s'invente pas la désaffection du sujet, du trouble, inexplicable volatilisation qui dévie son esprit — irrattrapable sans doute — rien n'est irrattrapable que ce que nous n'avons plus le goût de rattraper.

Il faudrait organiser les lignes d'une répétition — bénéficier de l'abracadabrante fantaisie de la stricte conformité ; mais les mots, ni les attentes, ni les regards, ni les gestes, ni les penchants, ni les absences ne seraient les mêmes.

Ni les décisions.

Elle avait le satanisme de savoir révéler la vertigineuse impudicité de la Femme.

Diamanterie des bourgeonnements
du tremble.

Le paisible philosophe s'alarmant, en le regrettant, que Vénus aimât l'opulence.

Qui pour moi s'interroge ? M'aimerait suffisamment pour capter mes effritements d'angoisse ? Me comprendrait à ma seule présence, ma seule forme, ma seule ombre ? M'aurait si précisément défini que je pourrais avoir l'apparence d'un enfant dans le premier âge ?

Qui ?

L'observateur : MOI.

Ainsi suis-je sur le point de dangereusement me méconnaître ; agissant à rebours de mes naturelles perspectives ; me choisissant en qualité d'ennemi préféré ; tournant ostensiblement le dos au bonheur proposé.

Me haïssant.

Je convoite ma réconciliation.

Upon waking—emptiness, no longer even your shape. My anxiety and uneasiness call out to you, but I am voiceless.

The subject invents itself—what doesn't invent itself is the withdrawal of the subject, of the unease, an inexplicable volatilization deviating—probably irretrievable—thought. Nothing is irretrievable except whatever we've lost the taste for retrieving.

It would be good to outline a repetition—to benefit from the preposterous fantasy of a strict correspondence; but neither the words, nor the expectations, nor the gazes, nor the gestures, nor the penchants, nor the absences would be the same.

Nor the decisions.

She was satanic enough to know how to reveal a Woman's breathtaking shamelessness.

The aspen's
bud-diamond factory.

The peaceful philosopher alarmed at, and deploring, Venus's love for opulence.

Who wonders about me? Would love me enough to notice whenever anxiety is eating away at me? Would understand me through my mere presence, my mere shape, my mere shadow? Would have defined me so precisely that I could look like a baby?

Who?

The observer: ME.

I am thus on the brink of dangerously misknowing myself; acting in the opposite direction from my natural perspectives; choosing myself as a favorite enemy; ostentatiously turning my back to the happiness offered.

Hating myself.

I covet my reconciliation.

Sa fuite soudaine dans les rues brûlantes de l'été.
Ne reste d'elle à la mémoire qu'un bouillonnement de tissus verts.

Aimer est une route.

Mer — paume lisse.
Musicalement accordée au soleil.
Ce que je prends de toi dans le creux de ma main ôte-t-il à ta vastitude, à ton poids ?
Quel est celui qui, sur tes autres bords, également au même instant se penche, te soustrayant cette poignée d'eau ?
Mer — connaissance commune.

Jamais je ne suis que l'essai de moi-même.

Ce fou désir *d'amour*.

Fleur de mouron —
étincelle bleue
dans le vernis de l'herbe verte.

— Êtes-vous aimé ?
— Je le suis.
— Comment le savez-vous ?
— On me le dit.
— Quelle inconséquence !
— À quoi d'autre jugez-vous de l'amour ?
— Je ne suis pas aimé.
— Quelle incongruité !

Her sudden flight down the burning hot streets of summer.
Only a boiling ferment of green cloth remains in memory.

Loving is a road.

Sea—smooth palm of the hand.
Musically in tune with the sun.
Does what I scoop up of you in the hollow of my hand take away from your vastness, your weight?
Who is that other person who, on one of your other shores, at this very moment, bends down and takes up this handful of water?
Sea—common knowledge.

I am never but the trying-out of myself.

This crazy craving for *love*.

Pimpernel flower—
blue spark
amid the polish of the green grass.

—Are you loved?
—I am.
—How do you know?
—I was told so.
—What inconsequence!
—By what else do you judge love?
—I am not loved.
—What incongruity!

Griffée au milieu de ma mémoire —
tu étais tous les degrés du Sexe équarrisseur.

En marchant de son pas glissant, elle se frotte aux murs chauds des arcades.
— Je fais l'amour à des passés de pierres.

Envol gris de la tourterelle.

Au-delà de la débauche dont elle vivait, sa façon désarmante de protéger en elle une part d'enfance. L'osmose, semblait-il, ne s'était pas accomplie entre l'enfant qu'elle avait été et la femme devenue ; prise, engluée dans les complexions du monde des hommes. Le regard clair était celui de l'intime candeur, la fraîcheur du visage, celle de l'incorruptibilité ; mais cette singulière, cette étourdissante association entre désinvolture et obscurité ténébreuse se faisait envoûtante ; paraissait lui appartenir le régime de l'existence — jusqu'à ce jour de fin d'automne qui la trouva morte sur son lit inondé de sang, la poitrine fracassée par la balle, les traits horriblement torturés. C'était une matinée mordorée ; bordant le lac, les allées du grand jardin qu'elle avait tant aimé commençaient à se pailleter de feuilles mortes.

Donnez des liqueurs fortes à celui qui périt
Et le vin à celui qui a l'amertume de l'âme
Qu'il boive et oublie sa pauvreté (Pr., XXXI, 6, 7).

Endors ton corps dans les mollesses du sable ; la mer nous est protectrice ; nous sommes l'un et l'autre dans cette étendue des centres apaisés, comme les produit la prière ; défais-toi de ta pensée, de toute supputation d'avenir ; sois égale, calme, uniquement allongée dans un moment sans attente.

Terra habitatur et quiescit

Like a claw scar in the middle of my memory—
you were all the steps in the Sex slaughterhouse process.

While gliding along, she rubs against the warm walls of the arcade.
—I make love to the pasts of stones.

Grayness of the turtledove taking flight.

Beyond the debauchery from which she earned her living, there was her disarming way of preserving a part of childhood inside her. Apparently, no osmosis had occurred between the little girl she had been and the woman she had become, now snared, bogged down in the intricacies of the world of men. Her clear gaze revealed her intimate candor, her fresh face showed her incorruptibility; but the singular, staggering association between heedless spontaneity and shadowy obscurity was bewitching; the entire scheme of existence seemingly belonged to her—until that end-autumn day when she was found dead on her blood-soaked bed, her chest shattered by a bullet, her facial features maimed from torture. It was a brown- and golden-tinted morning; along the lake, the walkways of the big park she had loved so much were beginning to be spangled with dead leaves.

Give strong drink unto him that is ready to perish,
And wine unto those that be of heavy hearts.
Let him drink, and forget his poverty (Proverbs 31: 6, 7).

Lull your body to sleep in the soft sand; the sea protects us; both of us are in this expanse of soothed centers, like those produced by prayer; undo your thoughts, any guessing at the future; be calm, even-tempered, just stretching out in a moment without expectations.

Terra habitatur et quiescit

Ce qui, seul, m'appartenait, gravement secret, soudain à toi révélé —
afin que tu disposes du point d'appui à l'aide duquel me connaître.
Que ce te soit une force
certitude
repos.
Me voilà dévalisé.
(Ensuite, je te porte — mais tes mystères ne sont que magma où nulle perspicacité ne saurait utilement s'insinuer.)

Pourquoi t'empressais-tu de devenir Femme ?

Incruster dans son regard les inouïes diversités du monde.

Liquéfaction appesantie d'après l'amour.

Commerce de Martial, le déchiqueteur :

> *Avec ton habit magnifique, Zoïle,*
> *tu te moques de mon habit râpé.*
> *Râpé, j'en conviens, mais il est à moi.*

Certains mots te ressemblent
certaines nuits de haute tension pétrifiée.
J'approche de toi
de gris, de noir, de rouge vêtue
tu me souris de tes yeux incertains.

Néron paya 6 000 sesterces deux petits vases de verre tant ces objets étaient de forme parfaite.

What alone belonged to me and was gravely secret was suddenly revealed to you—so that you would have a support to lean on, enabling you to know me.
May this be, for you, a force
certainty
rest.
Here I am, stripped of my belongings.
(After that, I carry you—but your mysteries are mere magma into which no perspicacity can usefully worm its way.)

Why were you in a hurry to become Woman?

Inlay the incredible diversities of the world into her gaze.

Weighty liquefaction after lovemaking.

Keeping company with Martial, the shredder:

> *Smart in a long-napped toga, you laugh, Zoilus,*
> *at my my threadbare garb.*
> *'Tis threadbare, no doubt, Zoilus, but 'tis my own.*

Certain words look like you
certain nights of petrified high tension.
As I approach
you are clothed in gray, black, and red
and smiling at me with your uncertain eyes.

Nero paid 6000 sesterces for two glass vases because of their perfect shapes.

Atteindre l'ultime précision — mort.

Dans les ruelles asphyxiées de chaleur, sa jupe à deux mains relevée sur une nudité blanche.

L'appréhension du malheur l'incitait à refuser ce qui était susceptible de le lui rappeler ; ainsi n'eut-il jamais une pensée pour les disparus de son entourage.

— Tout cela qui ne t'atteint pas n'est en substance rien puisque seule tu es mon inquiétude.
— Je me dispense de te connaître dans tes mensonges.
— Je ne m'éclaire que d'impossibilités.
— Quant à moi ?
— Je ne suis pas opposé à la distraction.

Polyphème dit :
— Clarté ! — les dieux ont figure du Jour.

Avance vers tes contraires. Édifie-toi protestataire contre ce qui te porte, te soutient, t'enlève à toi-même. Fais-toi indivisible subtilité, approfondissement de la connaissance. Entre dans la partie réservée du monde. Tu n'es admis qu'à la parcellisation. Qu'elle te devienne bien inaliénable. Partie du monde tienne, de ton unique éclairement, à ta seule ressemblance. Instaure-toi découverte et, de la sorte, conçois tes approches, tes encerclements. Consacre-toi à ton isolement. Point tant ne s'agit de grandeur que d'*étendue*.

Pelotonnée dans la chaleur du lit, enfantine retrouvée, elle remue en pensée des images qui ont ma silhouette.

Attain the ultimate precision—death.

In the suffocating hot lanes, her skirt lifted with both hands above her white nakedness.

Fearing misfortune prompted him to reject whatever was likely to make him recall it; he therefore never had a thought for those who had vanished from his circle.

—All this leaving you untouched is essentially nothing because only you are my uneasiness.
—I refrain from knowing you through your lies.
—Only impossibilities cast light on me.
—As for me?
—I am not opposed to distraction.

Polyphemus says:
—Clarity!—the gods look like the Day.

Head toward what is contrary to you. Build yourself up by protesting against what carries you, supports you, removes you from yourself. Make yourself into indivisible subtlety, deepening knowledge. Enter the private part of the world. You are admitted only to the parceling out. May your part become an inalienable good for you. A part of your own world, of your unique illumination, resembling you alone. Institute yourself as discovery and, in that way, plan your approaches, your encirclements. Devote yourself to your isolation. Greatness is much less the matter than *vastness*.

Snuggled into the warm bed, childlike once again, she stirs images in her mind that have my silhouette.

Langoureuse agonisante du plaisir.
Visage que tu ne te connais pas.
Basculement dans le dénuement de ta vérité profonde.
Brutale révélation incomprise.
Je t'observe — possédée et dépossédée.
Possédée et dépossédante.
Tu me deviens insecte disséqué.
Je pourrais te créer des formes et des noms inédits.
Corps assassinés.
Je souris.

Mer — ancienneté.
J'amène à ton baptême lustral des femmes jeunes, jolies.
Je t'offre des formes qui sont ta moulure.
Des corps grillonnés de désirs.
Marche de joyeuse acceptation du plaisir.
Nuit de caresses ensevelissantes.
Mains, cuisses, seins, reins, ventres, bouches, sexes.
Les lèvres sont d'éternelles inhumations voluptueuses.
J'aime la clarté acérée des sacrifices.

Une rose te précédait.

Venise — *ville de cloches et d'églises*, brusquement se noie dans une obscurité de glaise. Les grands palais sont énigmatiques.

Approche-toi. Dans cette riche quiétude, je te lirai ce que, jadis, fut l'habit moral d'une dame selon les couleurs : *Tout premièrement, dame ou demoiselle doit avoir ses pantoufles de couleur noire, qui dénote simplicité ; ce qui démontre aux dames qu'elles doivent marcher en toute simplicité et non en orgueil. Et, en après, la dame, de quelque état qu'elle soit, doit porter les jarretières qui seront de blanc et de noir, dénotant ferme propos de persévérer en vertu ; et ainsi que le blanc et le noir jamais ne change naturellement. Après ces choses, la cotte doit être d'un damas blanc, qui démontre l'honnêteté et chasteté qui doivent être en une dame ; idem doit être la pièce du devant, soit de couleur cramoisie, qui sera appelée la pièce de bonnes pensées ardentes envers Dieu.*

Languorous woman dying of pleasure.
Face you don't know as your own.
Toppling over into your bared deep truth.
Misunderstood brutal revelation.
I observe you—possessed and dispossessed.
Possessed and dispossessing.
You become a dissected insect for me.
I could create new shapes and names for you.
Assassinated bodies.
I smile.

Sea—ancientness.
I bring young beautiful women to your purifying baptism.
I offer you shapes fitting your mold.
Bodies cricketed with desires.
Walking marked by joyous acceptance of pleasure.
Night of enshrouding caresses.
Hands, thighs, breasts, lower backs, stomachs, mouths, sexual organs.
Lips are eternal voluptuous burials.
I like the keen clarity of sacrifices.

A rose went before you.

Venice—*city of bells and churches*, suddenly drowns in a clayish obscurity. The great palaces are enigmatic.

Approach. In this rich quietude, I'll read to you the description of what, formerly, was the morally decent clothing of a lady according to colors: *First and foremost, a lady or maiden lady should have black slippers, which signifies simplicity; which shows ladies that they should stroll simply, not haughtily. And then, whatever her standing, a lady should wear white and black garters, signifying a firm intention to persevere in virtue; and thus that white and black never change naturally. After these items, the cotte should be of white damask, which demonstrates the honesty and chastity that behooves a lady; the same should be true of the piece of clothing up front; that is, crimson in color, which will be called the piece of ardent good thoughts toward God.*

Enfin la robe, pour une grande dame, doit être de drap d'or, qui représente beau maintien ; car, tout ainsi que l'or plaît à la vue de chacun, à soi pareillement, le beau maintien d'une dame est cause qu'elle est prisée et regardée.

Moi, qui, seul, te peux concevoir.
T'accueillir dans ta simplicité.
T'admettre dans tes fabuleuses extravagances.
Hors moi, l'incertitude, le hasardeux, l'occasionnel.
Quel destin étrange à prétendre t'éloigner ?

Le Soleil est miroir flamboyant.

> *Les couleurs que la terre étale à nos yeux sont des signes manifestes pour celui qui pense.*

Marche dans ces jardins solaires, sereine, sûre de ta beauté.
Marche dans ces paradis de fleurs.
La Rose rouge a sens de pureté.

Ecce Adam, quasi unus ex nobis factus est, sciens bonum et malum.

Polyphème ferme son œil, aveugle de sa propre nuit.

Leurre des équivalences.

Poids de la terre. Masse incommensurable. Chape du désir.
Les corps sont offerts dans leur vulnérable opacité.
Viens — que je te soulage — qu'ensemble nous nous soulagions.
Que, par contradiction, nous apprenions l'élévation.
Qu'avant de retourner à notre boue, nous franchissions des degrés d'éther.

Finally the gown for a great lady should be made of golden cloth, which represents graceful bearing; for even as gold pleases everyone's eyes, and similarly oneself, the graceful bearing of a lady causes her to be valued and admired.

    I who alone can conceive you.
    Gather you in—in your simplicity.
    Accept you in all your fabulous extravagances.
    Beyond me: uncertainty, risk, random chance.
    What a strange destiny to wish to distance you?

    The Sun is blazing mirror.

> *The colors that the earth spreads*
> *before our eyes are obvious signs*
> *for the thinker.*

    Stroll serenely, confident in your beauty, in these sunny gardens.
    Stroll in these flower paradises.
    The red Rose has the sense of purity.

Ecce Adam, quasi unus ex nobis factus est, sciens bonum et malum.

    Polyphemus closes his eye, blind to his own night.

    Lure of equivalences.

    Weight of the earth. Incommensurable mass. Laden with desire.
    Bodies are offered in their vulnerable opaqueness.
    Come—so that I may relieve you—so that together we may relieve ourselves.
    So that, through contradiction, we learn how to elevate ourselves.
    So that, before returning to our mud, we rise through the levels of ether.

Ce que tu cherches avec tant de folie, dans une telle complexion d'erreurs n'est rien d'autre que l'absence de toi.
Une entente secrète t'autorise à être Ange.
Tu le sais depuis le premier jour de ton adolescence.
Mais les Paradis ne s'ouvrent pas à tout visiteur.

Dis-moi, Leslie, la couleur de Londres aujourd'hui ? . . .

Tu n'as pas vieilli ni ne vieilliras dans ce qui, en moi, m'ouvre à la vie.

Dieu n'apparaît qu'imparfaitement à Moïse,
lui dissimulant sa face.
Le dialogue a lieu dans une espèce d'abstraction tragique.

Rien ne nous retient
libertés en instance.

Te choisir, c'est m'annexer.

Dans l'herbe haute, les petites filles bleues chantent une comptine.

Sage chinois, Mencius dit : « La brebis n'était pas plus coupable que le bœuf ; c'est là un subterfuge de l'humanité. »

Pensée sans émotion ?
Ensemble du réseau nerveux dynamique.
Tenter la fragmentation — désir maléfique.
« Pensée pure » — est pensée qu'à fourni l'émotion qui, ensuite, s'efforce de s'en dégager.
« Pensée pure » — ne peut l'être que dans les conséquences.

What you seek so madly, making so many intricate mistakes, is nothing but your own absence.

A secret agreement authorizes you to be an Angel.

You have known this from the first day of your adolescence.

But Paradises don't open their gates to all visitors.

Tell me, Leslie, what color is London today?...

You neither have aged nor will age in what, inside me, opens me up to life.

God only partly appears before Moses,
for He covers His face.
The dialogue takes place in a kind of tragic abstraction.

Nothing retains us
freedoms are pending.

Choosing you means annexing myself.

In the high grass, the little blue girls are singing a nursery rhyme.

Mencius, the Chinese wise man, said: "The sheep was not guiltier than the ox; this is one of mankind's ploys."

Thought without emotion?
The whole dynamic nerve network.
To attempt fragmentation—a malefic desire.
"Pure thought"—is thought furnished by an emotion that subsequently tries to free itself from it.
"Pure thought"—can exist only in consequences.

Afin qu'elle soit, ma vie d'aujourd'hui est un jour supplémentaire de mémoire.

La nuit, vous pouvez vous approcher de vos femmes, qui sont votre vêtement, et vous le leur, dit le Prophète.

Elle avait l'élégance d'un grand oiseau calme.

Sa joliesse heureuse était frémissement.
Au-delà, se profilait la Femme ; qui décide, mesure, pèse, suppute, choisit.
L'enchantement consistait à regarder quelque peu en arrière.
Indéfinissable produit d'enfance et de proche connaissance.
Désir indécis de se tenir dans l'irresponsabilité, mais avidité d'agir.
On pouvait encore lui décerner tous les noms de l'émotivité exaltée.
Elle commençait à vivre dans une rue passante de Londres.

Droite et nue dans la chambre aux tentures mordorées.

Je me suis couché dans le lieu
des peaux divines, renversé
en présence de la déesse Shesat.

Endormi dans sa fourrure rousse, le chat sait où situer ma présence — sa pensée me suit.

Violence, forcer, maîtriser, oppresser, despotisme, intolérance, coercition, ordres impératifs.
Dans le printemps nouvellement épanoui, la première fleur rose, modeste, d'une exemplaire résistance.
Le viol la peut détruire, point l'anéantir.
Le tendre vent du matin balaie pour la journée ce qui doit l'être.

So that it may exist, my life today is an extra day of memory.

It is made lawful for you to go unto your wives on the night of the fast. They are raiment for you, and ye are raiment for them, says the Prophet.

She had the elegance of a big calm bird.

Her beaming prettiness was pure quivering.
Beyond this, Woman stood out; deciding, measuring, weighing, calculating, choosing.
The enchantment consisted in her looking somewhat backwards.
An indefinable product of childhood and close acquaintance.
A hesitant desire to maintain herself in irresponsibility, yet eager to act.
She could still be called by all the names of exalted emotiveness.
She began to live in a busy street of London.

Standing naked in the room with its lustrous bronze drapery.

> *I lay down in the room*
> *covered with divine hides, prostrate*
> *in the presence of the goddess Seshat.*

Asleep inside its auburn fur, the cat knows where to locate my presence—its thought follows me.

Violence, forcing, mastering, oppressing, despotism, intolerance, coercion, absolute orders.
In the newly radiant spring, the first rose blossom is modest, exemplarily resistant.
Rape can destroy it, but not annihilate it.
The tender wind of morning sweeps away, for the day, what must be swept away.

Temps mort, enfoui, piétiné, sans plus de consistance compréhensible ni de liens logiques ; temps du non-parlé, de la non-réponse ; absolu éthéré qui, cependant, peut-être, se prépare à la technique des conjonctions ; vers quel point précis de réalisation se diriger en ayant tout à coup conscience que j'y pourrais devenir *signe* ?

Je contemple longuement la morte sur son lit aux linges livides. Comment supposer que le rougeoiement de la vie ne serait que forme ? Silence, immobilité, sommeil ne sont en rien des substituts — le Souffle a fonction de rassemblement.

La morte étendue sur son petit lit étroit n'est ni vie ni mort encore — elle est objet, extérieurement intact.

Je cherche le nom, le son prodigieux de la mécanique interne ; toutefois sachant que des ramifications étrangères sans mots sont de vraies communications prolongées — jusqu'à l'assoupissement de toute mémoire.

Ailleurs, le monde est agitation, c'est-à-dire progression vers une nécessité de faire, davantage que l'espérance sans calcul prouvé, mais proprement certitude *de ce qui est*.

Ouvre ta bouche et je la remplirai

Ingrid revient de l'école . . .

Obtenir de soi l'impossible.

Chantonnant, l'enfant compte :
— 1, 2, 3, 4, 5 . . .
et ne sait plus ensuite. Il recommence :
— 1, 2, 3, 4, 5 . . .
sautant sur un pied
— 1, 2, 3, 4, 5 . . .
Ses yeux sont d'un troublant bleu pur.

A lull buried away, trampled on, with no more comprehensible substance or logical links; a time of no words spoken, no answers given; an ethereal absolute which nonetheless, perhaps, prepares itself for the technique of conjunctions; toward which precise point of realization should I head, suddenly aware that I could become a *sign* there?

I long contemplate the dead woman on her bed with its livid linen. How is it possible to imagine that the reddish glow of life would be only form? Silence, motionlessness, and sleep are by no means substitutes—Breath has a gathering function.

The dead woman lying on her little narrow bed is neither life nor death yet—she is an object, intact on the outside.

I seek the name, the prodigious sound of the inner mechanics; all the while knowing that wordless unknown ramifications are genuine kinds of prolonged communication—until all memory dulls.

Elsewhere, the world is agitation; that is, progression toward a necessity of doing, more than it is hope whose proof cannot be given and, indeed, the certitude *of what is.*

> *Open thy mouth wide and I will fill it*

Ingrid comes home from school . . .

Draw out the impossible from oneself.

Singing to himself, the child counts:
—1, 2, 3, 4, 5 . . .
and doesn't know how to continue. He begins again:
—1, 2, 3, 4, 5 . . .
hopping on one foot
—1, 2, 3, 4, 5 . . .
The pure blue color of his eyes is troubling.

La maison a ta chaleur, ta forme, tes emportements, tes débouchés, tes appétits.
La maison est l'une de tes textures accidentellement avouée.

Le Printemps est vert, rouge l'Été, bleu l'Automne, noir est l'Hiver.
Mets tes moufles, ton bonnet de laine — la neige est blanche.

On garde pour soi les mots.

Dans l'escalier de l'immeuble, quelqu'un monte d'un pas fatigué, répétant le mot allemand : *Kloster*.

Je partis tôt, avec mon chien,
Et m'en allai voir l'océan.
Les sirènes, des profondeurs,
Sortaient pour me regarder.

Quel précieux cristal ont-elles vu, douce, recouvrante, énigmatique Emily ?

Dans le luxueux hôtel étranger calfeutré par le poids de soie mauve des doubles rideaux du grand salon, assise légèrement dans un fauteuil, elle était l'image gravée de la *Présence*.
Il ne venait pas à l'idée qu'on pût lui adresser la parole, qu'on osât troubler son silence.

Matinées ensoleillées de Londres la frileuse
nous partagions nos découvertes
qui nous étaient langage.

The house has your warmth, your shape, your fits of anger, your outlets, your appetites.
The house is one of your textures, accidentally avowed.

Spring is green, Summer red, Autumn blue, Winter black.
Put on your mittens, your wool bonnet—the snow is white.

One keeps words to oneself.

Someone wearily walks up the stairway of the apartment building, repeating the German word *Kloster*.

> *I started Early—Took my Dog—*
> *And visited the Sea—*
> *The Mermaids in the Basement*
> *Came out to look at me.*

Sweet, enveloping, enigmatic Emily, what precious crystal did the mermaids see?

In the luxurious foreign hotel made cozy by the heavy mauve double silk curtains of the great receiving room, she was the graven image of *Presence* as she sat lightly in an armchair.
It crossed no one's mind to speak to her or disturb her silence.

Sunny mornings in shivering London
we shared our discoveries
that were a language for us.

Comptez-moi pour accident temporel ; j'œuvre différemment de moi vers ce qui peut obtenir la durée.
Un sourire dédaigneux vient à bout de tout.

Jeunes filles multicolores.

Sans cesse dissemblable
un permanent état de renouvellement
une permanente proportion d'inconnu
une constante progression reléguant l'autrui de la veille
l'éternelle jeunesse —
sans l'ennui.

Je ne redoute que mon ultime solitude.

Quelle qu'elle soit, je ne sais quoi d'amer la suit toujours (Properce).

Œil carmin dans le long vide de l'appartement
hiératique et soyeuse —
la Rose.

Je ne puis réfléchir avec ce qui n'est pas moi.

Je n'envie que ce qui m'empêche.

Éros loge dans l'effilement de ton corps, s'esclaffe par ton petit sexe ouvert, appelle, attire, tente, prometteur.
Éros te broie la pensée, la moud, la diversifie, la diminue, la dirige en tous sens, barattée jusqu'à ce que tu ne sois plus que ce toi-même qui ne se peut restreindre ; donné, concédé, jeté à la prise de l'autre ; de la sorte, tu es reine noire.

Consider me a temporal accident; I work in a different way from myself toward what can obtain duration.

A scornful smile gets to the end of anything.

Young multicolored girls.

Incessantly dissimilar
a permanent state of renewal
a permanent proportion of unknown elements
a constant progression relegating the other man from the day before
eternal youth—
without the boredom.

I dread only my ultimate solitude.

Whatever she is, something bitter always follows her. (Propertius).

Crimson eye in the long emptiness of the apartment—
silky and hieratic
the Rose.

I cannot think with what is not me.

I envy only what prevents me.

Eros lives in your slender body, bursts out laughing through your little open slit, calls out, attracts, tempts, seems promising.

Eros crushes your thoughts, grinds them, diversifies them, diminishes them, sends them off in all directions, churning them up until nothing remains of you except that you who can't restrain itself; given away, handed over, tossed toward the other's grasp; in this way, you're a black queen.

Cloche gaie — de la mort.

Entre deux êtres, l'entente a ceci de particulier qu'elle se refuse à la subtilité de la complication ; étrangère à la systématique opposition de la négation ; creusement en direction de l'égalisation, presque mimétisme.
L'entente est loi.

Matins de nos départs.
Tu es d'une exubérante jeunesse, d'une impressionnante assurance de la beauté.
Les trains sont nos alibis.

Mordre ce ciel à joue d'enfant.

Cheveux épars sur un coussin.

Peut-être étais-je ta recherche, mais le temps nous était contraire.
Reste dans ma mémoire avec tes minces tailleurs noirs, ta lingerie fine, tes jupes courtes et virevoltantes, tes déguisements d'enfant, tes foulards jetés sur les lampes des chambres pour en assourdir l'éclat.

Femmes qui vinrent à moi avec une puissance amoureuse offerte — et me protégèrent.

Infime corps de frissons verts, œil de soufre, qui guette ou s'endort.
Fin lézard dans l'écrasement du soleil.

Merry bell—of death.

What is special about mutual understanding between two human beings is that the subtleties of complication are rejected; that it remains foreign to negation used in systematic opposition; that it digs ever deeper toward equalization, almost toward mimesis.
The mutual understanding rules.

Mornings when we depart.
You are exuberantly youthful, impressively assured of beauty.
The trains are our alibis.

Bite this sky with its childlike cheeks.

Hair spread over a cushion.

Perhaps I was what you were searching for, but time was against us.
Remain in my memory with your tight-fitting black outfits, your sheer lingerie, your short twirling skirts, your childlike disguises, your scarves tossed over the bedroom lamps in order to dim the brightness.

Women who came to me, offering their amorous powers—and protected me.

Tiny green trembling body with its sulfurous eye sleeping or keeping watch.
Slender lizard in the sunlight beating down.

Dans un pays de l'Équateur existe une fleur à la fascinante beauté ; ses pétales ne s'ouvrent qu'avec le petit jour pour se refermer sous le grand soleil de la chaleur des étés ; elle est raidement dressée sur sa tige comme le serait un corps de femme dans un tissu moulant — son parfum est enivrant, celui de la mort.

Mer — qui n'est que retour.

Je t'habille, ville froide
ville anesthésiée
je te vêts de mes femmes en allées
soudainement si proches
féeriquement actives
traductrices des plus audacieuses pensées
en âmes soumises pour les grandes issues du plaisir
les renversements meurtriers
les assoupissements à goût de sang
tiens-toi aveugle et muette
ville mille fois chevauchée.

Force claire de l'Isolé.

Éternelle jeunesse.
Les attachements sont obstacles aux possibles.
Concept de liberté agissante, vouée à l'absorption des puissances vitales.
Je suis telle ou telle sorte de possibles ; autrement dit, je suis constitué pour occuper leurs plans.
Définition, délimitation de soi.
Au-delà, rêverie, espaces vagues, velléités, confusion des possibles concourant à un impossible affectif, improductif.
Je suis au cœur de l'espace des possibles — qui est à saisir, à se former à mon image. (Non pas choix, mais volonté d'appétence, de conquête, d'imprégnation.)
Je suis invité à l'incessant banquet du monde.
(À moi également de concevoir l'espace des possibles religieux.)

In an equatorial country there exists a fascinatingly beautiful flower; its petals open only at dawn, then close under the scorching sun of the hot summers; it stands stiffly on its stem as would the body of a woman in a tight-fitting garment—its scent is heady, that of death.

Sea—that is nothing but return.

I dress you, cold city
anesthetized city
clothe you with my women who have left
and are suddenly so near
active like fairies
translators of the most ardent thoughts
into souls subjected for the great outcomes of pleasure
the murderous upheavals
the drowsiness tasting like blood
stand there blind and speechless
city a thousand times straddled.

Clear force of the Loner.

Eternal youth.
Attachments are obstacles to possibilities.
Concept of active liberty, devoted to absorbing vital powers.
I am such and such a possibility; in other words, I have been put together in order to occupy their plans.
Definition, delimitation of self.
Beyond, reverie, vague spaces, vague impulses, the confusion of the possibilities working toward an unproductive, emotional impossibility.
I am at the heart of the space of possibilities—which is to be grasped and shaped in accordance with my own image. (Not choice, but willingness for appetency, conquest, impregnation.)
I am invited to the incessant banquet of the world.
(It is also up to me to imagine the space of religious possibilities.)

Polyphème s'inquiète :
— Quelle seras-tu, cruauté de mon destin ? Quel seras-tu, inconnu à venir, qui l'exécutera avec haine ? Qui m'aura deviné dans ma bonté de pasteur, mes doutes, mes tares ? Qui m'aura soupçonné dans mes peurs ?

Italie — depuis si longtemps morte.

Rues ensommeillées du matin.
Tu n'étais que rire.
Tu m'as laissé pour aller t'acheter une pomme verte.

Lilith, fille de la Terre —
de l'indistinct
du désarroi
des haines
des amours perdues
Lilith condamnée aux profondeurs neptuniennes afin que la Séduction ne devînt pas axe du monde
Lilith — la séparée.

La première heure, une Rose
La deuxième heure, un Héliotrope
La troisième heure, une Rose blanche
La quatrième heure, une Jacinthe
La cinquième heure, un Citron
La sixième heure, un Lotus
La septième heure, un Lupin
La huitième heure, une Orange
La neuvième heure, un Olivier
La dixième heure, un Peuplier
La onzième heure, un Souci
La douzième heure, une Violette
Vivre — constant ajustement.

Polyphemus is worried:
—What cruel destiny will you be? What unknown man will you be, coming to carry it out with hatred? Who will have made me out in my shepherd-like goodness, my doubts, my flaws? Who will have suspected me in my fears?

Italy—dead for such a long time.

Drowsy morning streets.
You were pure laughter.
You left me in order to buy a green apple for yourself.

Lilith, daughter of the Earth—
of indistinctness
of helplessness
of hatreds
of lost loves
Lilith sentenced to Neptunian depths so that Seduction would not become the main road of the world
Lilith—the woman kept apart.

The first hour, a Rose
The second hour, a Heliotrope
The third hour, a white Rose
The fourth hour, a Hyacinth
The fifth hour, a Lemon
The sixth hour, a Lotus
The seventh hour, a Lupin
The eighth hour, an Orange
The ninth hour, an Olive Tree
The tenth hour, a Poplar
The eleventh hour, a Marigold
The twelfth hour, a Violet
Living—constant adjustment.

Plaintes, sifflements, soupirs, douloureux murmures ; en brûlant, le bois pleure, corps massif, noirci, contorsionné, peut-être souffrant, contraire à lui-même, soudain étranger à sa force qui fut beauté, malmené, en torture ; néanmoins utile encore par sa désagrégation.

Idée de sacrifice, d'impressionnante pesanteur que nulle volonté ne saurait soustraire au progressif anéantissement.

Quelles vérités sont celles des Enfers ?

Interrogation — être — appartenir — se détruire —

Je suis mieux seul, car lorsque je suis seul, je suis avec Dieu (Vassili Rozanov).

Je me rencontre en clown.

— Il y a bien longtemps que personne n'est entré chez nous, dit-elle, détachant chacune de ses syllabes.

Les formes sont unifiées.

À quinze ans, Hermogène de Tarse fait par ses connaissances l'admiration de Marc Aurèle.

À vingt-cinq ans, il perd la mémoire et meurt à un âge avancé, après avoir traîné des années durant son cerveau mort.

L'enfant ne regarde pas — il *sait* ce qui est du registre de la Vie, de son développement.

Dans la grande chambre verte, si droite assise devant le miroir, tandis que, brumeuse, Londres s'ensomnole, les doigts délicatement défont ce ruban fauve qui noue la pesanteur de tes cheveux.

Groans, wheezing, sighs, painful murmurs; the log is weeping as it burns, its massive body blackened, writhing, perhaps suffering, no longer its own self, suddenly foreign to its force that once was beauty, ill-treated, tortured; nonetheless still useful in its disintegration.

Idea of sacrifice, of impressive gravity that no willpower would know how to remove from progressive annihilation.

What truths has Hell?

Interrogation—to be—to belong—to destroy oneself—

I am better alone, for when I am alone I am with God (Vassily Rozanov).

I meet myself as a clown.

—It has been a long time since anyone has come into our home, she says, pronouncing each syllable distinctly.

The forms are unified.

At the age of fifteen, Hermogenes of Tarsos wins the admiration of Marcus Aurelius because of his knowledge.

At the age of twenty-five, he loses his memory and dies in old age, having lugged his dead brain around for years.

A child doesn't look around—he *knows* what pertains to Life, to his development.

In the big green room, sitting up straight before the mirror while foggy London drowses off, you delicately use your fingers to undo the tawny ribbon knotting your thick hair.

Près de nous, ce soir, homme des plaisirs, qu'un colonel de son temps jugea « trop indolent, même pour l'armée », William Collins, le désespéré, qu'emporta la nuit de la confusion.

*The band, legends say,
was wove on that creating day*

Renverse vers moi ton beau visage.

Sur l'aquarelle de la largeur d'une main, la Femme est en robe du soir qui laisse à nu l'éclat rose de ses épaules, tandis qu'un noir profond prend les seins et la taille, qu'un rouge vaporeux est comme l'écorce souple du reste du corps.
Le bal va commencer.

Cette nuit-là, son sommeil fut néanmoins agité, rempli d'images de voyageurs arrivant dans sa grotte, destinés par les dieux à porter sur lui le Malheur.

Étoile secrète de la pomme.

Comment entendais-je ton regard ?

Suite de hasards prémédités appelés Temps.

Déperdition au milieu de *l'absent*.
L'habileté consisterait à posséder les moyens de *revenir*.
Nous sommes les démarcheurs du plein.

Near us this evening, William Collins, a man of pleasure whom a colonel back then judged "too indolent even for the army," a desperate man who was carried off by the darkness of mental confusion.

The band, as fairy legends say,
Was wove on that creating day.

Turn your beautiful face back toward me.

In a watercolor painting no larger than the width of a hand, the Woman is wearing an evening gown that reveals the rose sheen of her shoulders while deep black grasps her breasts and waist, and a vaporous red covers the rest of her body like soft bark.
The ball is about to begin.

That night, his sleep was nonetheless restless, full of visions of travelers entering his cave and destined by the gods to bring Misfortune down upon him.

The apple's secret star.

How did I hear your gaze?

Sequence of premeditated whims of chance that are called Time.

Wasting away amid what is *absent*.
Dexterity would mean possessing the means to *come back*.
We go from door to door canvassing for wholeness.

Shylock consent à prêter de l'argent sous convention de tailler dans son débiteur un poids convenu de chair s'il se trouve, au jour dit, dans l'incapacité de faire face à sa dette.

Le jour venu, toujours dépourvu de ressources, le malheureux s'adresse au tribunal afin d'échapper, s'il se peut, à la cruauté du marché, que le juge approuve, à condition toutefois que Shylock ne prélève en chair que selon son dû exact, au risque pour lui d'avoir autrement la tête tranchée ; menace lui inspirant la sagesse de renoncer à sa créance.

Magnétisme érotique qui te transfigure —
intouchable beauté figée
à la limite de deux dangereux passages.
Te suivre jusqu'à la consumation — ou s'agripper au tenace.

L'insecte à carapace écarlate posé comme un œil interrogateur sur la large feuille verte de la plante.

M'indiffère l'échéance. Peu me chaut ce factice partage. Je n'ai ni à emprunter ni à tracter. S'en tenir aux lois invariables de la raison n'offre à mon esprit qu'intérêt nul. Je me dissèque, m'exploite moi-même — n'en ramenant que ce qui me figure et qui, a ce titre, est d'une indéniable valeur — celle de l'exceptionnel. Je ne ressemble pas. La ressemblance est faux prétexte, leurre de commodité ; sans enseignantes divulgations. Vivre est immobile expansion. Je me reconnais à la mesure de ce que je puis me fournir en accélérations de pensée. L'heure venue de comprendre, je me détourne vers l'imprécis du sensible :

> *It will be Summer — eventually*
> *Ladies — with parasols*
> *Sauntering Gentlemen — with Canes —*
> *And little Girls — with Dolls.*

Un poème — et tout m'est révélé.

Shylock consents to lend money with the stipulation that he can carve out an agreed-upon weight of his debtor's flesh if, on the chosen day, the man is unable to settle his debt.

When the day comes, the hapless man, who still lacks financial means, appeals to the tribunal in order to avoid, if possible, the cruelty of this bargain, which the judge accepts, provided that Shylock deducts, in flesh, only the exact amount owed; otherwise he will be beheaded. The threat inspires him to be wise enough to abandon his pecuniary claim.

Erotic magnetism transfiguring you—
untouchable stilted beauty
at the limit of two dangerous passageways.
Either follow you until all is consumed—or cling to what resists the force.

The scarlet-carapaced insect positioned like an inquisitive eye on the big green leaf of the plant.

I couldn't care less about the deadline. Sham sharing matters little to me. I need neither to borrow nor to bargain. Keeping to the invariable laws of reason has no interest for my mind. I dissect myself, exploit my own self, bringing back only what represents me and, therefore, is undeniably valuable: what is rare. I don't look like. Looking like is a false pretext, a convenient illusion; without instructive disclosures. Living is motionless expansion. I recognize myself according to the accelerated thoughts with which I can furnish myself. When the moment comes to understand, I detour toward the imprecision of what is sensitive:

> *It will be Summer—eventually.*
> *Ladies—with parasols*
> *Sauntering Gentlemen—with Canes—*
> *And little Girls—with Dolls.*

A poem—and everything is revealed to me.

Ton domaine est la rue, la foule, la violence, la nuit ; animal de proie, qui cherche, hume ses prochaines victimes, à coup sûr les choisit pour la volonté de son plaisir.
Sorcière au visage d'enfant. Crispation du Sexe. Putain.

Tragique dépouillement de l'homme circonscrit à sa seule solitude : *Priez, afin que vous ne tombiez pas en tentation* (Luc, XXII, 40).

Ce qui s'épuise et meurt.

Grande salle décorative nue où, le soir tombé, tu te mettais en riant à mes genoux pour un simulacre de plaisir.

J'attends de me regarder pour être *inconnu*.

Se délivrer de ce qui n'est jamais qu'alignement depuis toujours pratiqué dans la lassitude irréfléchie de l'habitude ; dans la torpeur de l'inconscience moins même : dans la vacuité mécanique.
Se délivrer d'un enchaînement de mots qui n'ont pas force de création, volatils comme poussière ; mots de systèmes, de fabrications ponctuelles, rejetés aussitôt que formulés dans la quotidienne arène privée de vibrations.
Se délivrer de ce qui n'est pas voyance, magie, miracle.

Viser le fil tendu au-dessus du gigantesque danger.
Nous sommes éternelle Chute.

Venise — mort calme.
Leopardi traîne dans ma mémoire — *Le cœur humain, toujours trompé dans ses espoirs, est toujours prêt à se laisser tromper ; toujours déçu par l'espérance et toujours prêt à l'être ; non seulement ouvert à l'espoir, mais possédé par lui dans l'instant même du dernier désespoir, dans l'acte même du suicide.*

Your realm is the street, crowds, violence, night; an animal of prey who stalks, smells out her next victims, choosing them sure-handedly for her pleasure's will.

Witch with a childlike face. Tensed-up Sex. Slut.

Tragic asceticism of man wholly confined to his solitude: *Pray that ye enter not into temptation.* (Luke 22:40).

What gets exhausted and dies.

Big bare decorative room where, once night had fallen, you would laughingly position yourself in front of my knees for a simulacrum of pleasure.

I am waiting to gaze at myself in order to be *unknown*.

To free oneself from what is never but alignment ever carried out in thoughtless lassitude of habit; in the torpor of unconsciousness; even less: in mechanical vacuity.

To free oneself from a sequence of words having no creative force and volatile like dust; words of systems, specific fabrications, rejected as soon as they are formulated in the private daily arena of vibrations.

To free oneself from all that is not clairvoyance, magic, miracle.

Aim for the tightrope over the gigantic danger.
We are eternal Falling.

Venice—calm death.

Leopardi still roams in my memory—*Always deluded in its hopes, the human heart is always ready to let itself be deluded; always disappointed by hope and always ready to be so: not only open to hope, but possessed by it in the very moment of the final despair, in the very act of suicide.*

Ouvre ta bouche pour mon plaisir.
Venise — léthargique.

Ce quelque chose d'abolissant — qui est rencontre, double cohésion, effacement dans une réduction de l'unique ; consentement à une trajectoire anonyme sans plus de repères ni de véritable but — qui n'est que retour, régression.
Qu'as-tu à me dire, qui ne s'exprime que par les violences du corps ?
Cristal au bord de l'éclatement.
Corpo celestiale.

Par *désir de conciliation*, je m'obstine à argumenter contre moi-même, jusques et y compris dans les cas où il est d'évidence que je trace vers le vrai incontestable, ayant dénoyauté la série des questions contenant cette flammèche — que je laisse souffler par le premier venu.
Entre également dans cette attitude de la fatigue.
Ils ne savent pas, ne savent rien. L'explication est fastidieuse.
Les admettre est déjà un suffisant effort.

Étincellements. Robes volantes. Longue jambe noire. Profondeurs moites. Orées de tout inconnu. Pleurs. Enfantillages. Confessions. Terreurs.
Tu fus la largeur d'une main qui conduit ingénument dans les dédales prohibés.

Je te contemple, illogique, animale — douée d'énergies secrètes qui, dans ta fragilité, te construisent un monde.

— Qui suis-je ?
Paupières baissées.
— Jeu mortel.

Open your mouth for my pleasure.
Venice—lethargic.

This something that abolishes—this something that is encounter, double cohesion, effacement in a reduction of the unique; that is consent to an anonymous trajectory with no more landmarks and no genuine goal—this something that is nothing but return, regression.

What do you have to tell me that expresses itself only by bodily violence?

Crystal about to shatter.

Corpo celestiale.

Desiring conciliation, I keep stubbornly arguing against myself, even in cases where it is obvious that I am speeding toward uncontestable truths, having dissected the series of questions containing the flickering flame—which I let the first person to show up blow out.

Weariness also enters into this attitude.

They don't know, know nothing. Explaining is fastidious.

Letting them in already demands enough efforts.

Sparkles. Sweeping gowns. Long black leg. Moist depths. Edges of everything unknown. Weeping. Childishness. Confessions. Terrors.

You were the width of a hand ingenuously leading into the forbidden labyrinths.

I contemplate you in your illogicality, your animalism—a woman gifted with secret energies which, in your fragility, construct a world for you.

—Who am I?
Lowered eyelids.
—Deadly game.

Polyphème a fait un rêve atroce.

J'avais bu plus que de raison, je m'étais allongé pour dormir sur mes peaux, la tête me tournait un peu ; j'ai vu un étranger s'approcher de moi, m'observer comme s'il m'avait à sa merci et, en effet, je n'étais plus même en état de me remettre sur mes jambes ; soudain pris je ne sais où, il brandissait au-dessus de ma tête un long pieu dont je compris qu'il cherchait à m'aveugler en le plantant dans mon œil. Quelle horreur ! Je me suis réveillé en sursaut ; la nuque humide de transpiration.

Mer éternité.
(Je me penche et me vois dans des tourments anciens . . .)

Je te prends pour reposante image.

Silhouette noire qui, chaque matin à la même heure, circulait dans la neige entre l'hôtel et la clinique de montagne.

Elle n'avait de complicité qu'avec l'obscur, le compromis, la décomposition.
L'outrance du soleil confinait pour elle à l'enténèbrement, à quoi elle se complaisait.
Son impatience à sombrer dans les faillites du corps.

Comment me retrouverez-vous, vous qui ignorez où je vis, vous à qui jamais je n'ai eu encore le temps de dire mon nom, vous que jamais je n'ai vu, à qui je m'adresse dans mon désarroi afin d'obtenir sans savoir si je le mérite ce que je demande.
Comment me retrouverez-vous — ensemble et séparés ?

Nuits insomniaques rituellement consacrées aux malignités de ton corps.

Polyphemus has had an atrocious dream.
—I had drunk more than was reasonable and sprawled out to sleep on my hides, my head spinning a little. I saw a stranger approaching, watching me as if he had me at his mercy and, indeed, I was not in a condition to get back up on my feet; suddenly brandishing over my head a long stake picked up from who knows where, he was trying—so I understood—to blind me by thrusting it in my eye. How horrible! I awoke with a start, my neck sweaty.

Sea—eternity.
(I bend down and see myself in former torments . . .)

I take you for a restful image.

Dark silhouette who, every morning at the same hour, trekked through the snow between the hotel and the mountain clinic.

She had complicity only with darkness, compromise, decay.
The excessive sun confined her to shadows in which she took pleasure.
Her impatience to sink into the failures of the body.

How will you both find me, you who don't know where I live, to whom I still haven't had the time to tell my name, whom I've never seen, to whom I appeal in my helplessness in order to obtain what I'm asking though not knowing whether I deserve it.
How will you find me—will you be together and separate?

Insomniac nights ritually devoted to the malice of your body.

Que l'être proche aimé vous soit en garde
Que le jour resplendisse
Que soit répandue la splendeur des fleurs
Que le faible insecte trouve son chemin parmi les obstacles d'herbe et de pierres
Qu'en se polissant d'eau de pluie la pierre s'embellisse
Que ce qui a froid se réchauffe
Que les oiseaux rassurés viennent picorer devant la maison
Que le Mal soit avec fermeté contenu dans la nuit caïnite
Que partout la clarté soit maîtresse
Que l'amour sache son nom et sa puissance
Que du temps soit accordé à la tendresse
Que les démons souterrains ne brisent pas leur enveloppe
Que l'oiseau rouge chante
Que le soleil nous enseigne le sens du bienheureux repos
Que le ciel soit un espace d'images somnolentes
Que la main soit accueillante
Que le chien m'escorte de ses gambades heureuses
Que la maison soit douce, acceptante
Que tu sois présente jusqu'à mon dernier endormissement.
Prière.

Mystique de l'amour
de l'érotisme
vouloir plus ou moins conscient d'un commun territoire de transcendance.

Profondeur de cuir des larges fauteuils proches l'un de l'autre.
Odeur d'alcool des verres servis, de son parfum acide et doux.
Bouleversante musique nécromancienne de Vivaldi.
Bruissement des regards.
Jambe jeune enveloppée du nuage bistre du bas.
Corolle souple de la robe.
Intensité des désirs en attente.
À nos fenêtres, Londres frotte son museau gris.

May whomever you love watch over you
May the day shine
May the splendor of flowers spread
May the weak insect find its path among the grass and stone obstacles
May the stone be embellished by the polishing of rainwater
May whatever feels cold warm up
May reassured birds come to peck in front of the house
May Evil be firmly contained in the Cainitic night
May clarity be the mistress everywhere
May love know its name and its power
May time be devoted to tenderness
May the underground demons not break out of their wrappings
May the red bird sing
May the sun teach us the meaning of blessed rest
May the sky be an expanse of drowsy imagery
May the hand invite
May the dog escort me, happily frisking about
May the house be gentle, welcoming
May you be present until I fall asleep for the last time
Prayer.

Mystic of love
of eroticism
the more or less conscious desire for a common territory of transcendence.

Leathery depths of the big armchairs next to each other.
The smell of alcohol rising from the served glasses, the sweet acidic fragrance.
Vivaldi's deeply moving necromantic music.
Glances rustling.
Young leg enveloped in the swarthy haze of a nylon stocking.
Lithesome corolla of the dress.
Intensity of desires in waiting.
At our windows, London rubs its gray snout.

L'enchantement tenait à ce que, ensemble, nous instituions des ailleurs exempts des collusions du réel.

Il n'y a plus d'heure — mais un temps passif, une voûte d'accueil à ce qui n'était plus *que le désir*.

Tranchées impossibles à renouveler.

J'avais pour nous choisi d'être parallèles.

Comme ta joliesse avait choisi de se consacrer exclusivement à elle-même.

Nous appartenions à une dilatation de la pression fantasmagorique.

Nous avions trouvé l'exact équilibre du voyageur.

Élégance discrète de cet ensemble à pantalon blanc qui, dans ce grand café de province, était un écrin dessinant de toi la Femme future.

Dévoré d'amour pour toi, j'aurais voulu pouvoir indéfiniment prolonger cet après-midi de douce grisaille, étonné que tu ne devines rien de ce qui me bouleversait.

Danse. Nuit. Exacerbation. Excitation. Possession. Refus. Égotisme. Nuit. Danse. Nuit.

Le trouble émanant d'elle provenait de sa pureté vipérine.

Séduction ophidienne.

Auréole solaire d'une petite goutte de sang.

Limitation
        Empêchement
                Mort

Règles, réduction des puissances absorbantes de la pensée

Exclu qui ne croit pas à l'effusion.

The enchantment depended on whether we together instituted elsewheres exempt of the collusions of reality.

There is no more time on the clock—only a passive period, an archway welcoming what was no longer anything *but desire*.

Trenchways impossible to renew.

For us, I had decided we would be parallel.

Even as your prettiness had decided to care exclusively for itself.

We belonged to a dilatation of phantasmagoric pressure.

We had found the exact equilibrium of the *traveler*.

Discrete elegance of that outfit with its white pants which, in the big provincial café, was a shapely showcase for you as the Future Woman.

Devoured by my love for you, I wanted to prolong indefinitely that sweet grayish afternoon, surprised that you were noticing nothing of what was moving me.

Dance. Night. Exacerbation. Excitement. Possession. Refusal. Egotism. Night. Dance. Night.

The turmoil she exuded came from her viperine purity.
Ophidian seduction.

The solar halo of a little drop of blood.

Limitation
        Hindrance
                Death
Rules, reduction of the absorbing powers of thought
Anyone not believing in effusion is excluded.

Te commencer. Te perdre. Te façonner. Te défaire. T'ouvrir les portes réservées. Les refermer à ta nouvelle approche. Tu m'as été. Tu ne peux m'être. Te consolider dans mes rêves extravagants. Te perdre dans leur dilution. Te projeter. Te ramener et te quitter. T'auréoler. Te réduire à ta propre dimension.

Il existe un jeu composé d'une bobine à deux cônes opposés par les sommets, qu'on lance en l'air et qu'on rattrape au moyen d'une longue ficelle souple ou tendue entre deux baguettes de bois.

Ce jeu s'appelle diabolo — du nom grec du Diable : diabolos.

Point tant n'est-il question que d'être en accord avec des expressions non toujours forcément contrôlées, mais plutôt s'agit-il de susciter de possibles champs d'accord.

En ce cas, l'art est terrain privilégié.

Il ne peut alors être question que de Centre ; sans oublier que celui-ci se déplace et, qu'à nous-mêmes, nous sommes Centre. (D'où l'éruption de la poésie, qui ne s'accommode que d'essentiel.)

Je ne suis pas en représentation.

Le visage à demi baissé, le pas fuyant, quelqu'un dans l'obscurité s'approche afin de désigner du doigt celui qui doit être sacrifié.

Quelle est la couleur, la résonance de l'instant où il prend conscience de l'irréparable étendue de son acte ?

Qui sera-t-il alors, sinon l'éternel réprouvé ?

Mais de quelle puissance son obligation dénonciatrice — de quel service ?

Il se pleure lui-même dans son exclusion.

Lames en bouquets des feuilles de tulipes.

To begin you. To lose you. To fashion you. To take you apart. To open private doors for you. To close them when you approach again. You were me. You cannot be me. To consolidate you in my extravagant dreams. To lose you in their dilution. To project you. To bring you back and to leave you. To glorify you with a halo. To reduce you to your own dimension.

There's a game involving a spool shaped by two cones joined at their apices. The spool is tossed into the air and then caught by means of a long loose or taut string held between two wooden sticks.

This game is called diabolo—from the Greek name for the Devil: diabolos.

The problem is not so much to be in agreement with not always necessarily verified expressions, but rather to give rise to possible fields of agreement.

Art offers a privileged realm for this.

Only the Center thus matters; not to forget that the Center shifts and that we are Centers for ourselves. (Whence the surging forth of poetry, which accommodates itself only to what is essential.)

I represent nothing, play no role.

With his head half-bowed, a man evasively steps forward from the darkness in order to point to the person who must be sacrificed.

What is the color, the resonance of the moment when he becomes aware of the irreparable consequences of his act?

Who will he thereafter be, save the eternal reprobate?

But from what authority does this obligation to denounce come—from what mission?

He weeps for himself in his exclusion.

Blades gathered into bouquets of tulip leaves.

C'est une petite ville inconnue de nous. Nous y sommes des étrangers. On nous observe en conséquence. Nous parcourons les rues au pas de promenade. Il y a une église romane. Pureté féminine. À l'intérieur, un beau Christ de bois, une Vierge revêtue d'un long manteau blanc, comme une jeune mariée. Le soleil entre par la porte ouverte. Tu pries avec profondeur. Ton profil est d'une tranquille noblesse. Au bout d'une rue droite en pente, il y a une rivière à l'eau verte transparente. Nous n'en connaissons pas le nom. Nous sommes libres parmi les choses qui se présentent elles-mêmes dans leur authenticité, leur poids naturel. Les passants ont un pain sous le bras, ou planté dans un cabas. Une terrasse est accueillante sur une place aux dimensions d'un décor de théâtre. Nous mangeons du poisson de rivière. Nous buvons du vin blanc très clair, sec. Nous sommes vivants, dans un espace du monde. J'aime la couleur irisée de ton rouge à lèvres.

— Qu'attends-tu de moi ?
— Que tu ne t'identifies plus que sous mes angoisses.
— Ma dépossession ?
— T'annuler — te dénaître.
— Est-ce morte que tu me veux ?
— Vivante, mais supprimée.

Écartement des cuisses dans le tissu transparent de la jupe tendue.

Fleur séchée
étrangeté de la beauté transformée.

L'opposé d'une somme est la somme des opposés.
(*Tes yeux sont des égrènements verts.*)

Araignée noire.
À demi étendue dans le fauteuil de chintz rouge.
— Je pense à un corps d'homme.

We've never visited this small town. We're strangers here. We're watched accordingly. We stroll through the streets. There is a Romanesque church. Feminine purity. Inside, a beautiful wooden Christ and a Virgin covered with a long white cloak as if she were a young bride. Sunlight shines through the open door. You're deep in prayer. Seen from the side, you exude quiet nobility. At the bottom of a straight, downward sloping street flows a stream with transparent green water. We don't know its name. We're free among things that come forward in their genuineness, with their natural weight. The passersby have bread loaves under their arms or stuck in shopping bags. A café terrace seems inviting on a square the size of stage scenery. We eat river fish. We drink a pale, dry, white wine. We're alive in a part of the world. I love the iridescent color of your lipstick.

—What do you expect of me?
—That you henceforth identify yourself only in accordance with my anxieties.
—My dispossession?
—To nullify you—to take away your birth.
—Do you thus want me as a dead woman?
—Alive, but done away with.

Thighs spread beneath the transparent cloth of the tight skirt.

Dry flower
strangeness of transformed beauty.

The opposite of a sum is the sum of its opposites.
(*Your green eyes are shelled grain.*)

Black spider.
She's half stretched out in the red chintz armchair.
—I am thinking of a man's body.

Parfois aussi, pourquoi ne pas l'admettre ? les trouvailles de l'imbécillité m'enchantent.

Éliminer. Circonscrire. Condenser à une naturelle nécessité. Devenir est déjà accompli.

Elle n'était que riches chaussures, flot de tissus bariolés.
Corps menu qui était son luxe.
Jetée sur les draps blancs, ses lèvres d'une épaisseur obsédante, obscène.
Elle parlait pour elle-même, sa voix endormie au fond de ce corps que dévastait le désir.
Trop présente elle était inapprochable.

Geoffroy de Rudel, bien qu'il ne la connaisse pas, s'éprend de la comtesse de Tripoli d'après les récits faits sur elle par les pèlerins qui revenaient d'Antioche ; il trouve plusieurs chansons en son honneur, puis se fait croisé pour la voir ; mais il est atteint sur le vaisseau d'une maladie si grave que tous le considèrent comme mort. On parvient cependant à le conduire à Tripoli, où il est déposé dans une hôtellerie ; informée aussitôt de son arrivée, la comtesse accourt embrasser son amant inconnu, qui reprend connaissance, remercie Dieu d'avoir conservé ses jours jusqu'à ce moment et rend le dernier soupir. La comtesse elle-même prit le voile, de la douleur qu'elle en ressentit.

Gaïa — débordement de fécondité lourde.
Gaïa — nourriture de la mort.

Incertain, son jeune corps comme à l'offrande dans le froissement des étoffes noires.
Enfance tentatrice.
Abîmes de la Femme.
Désirant la mort et son désir.

Why not admit it? Sometimes I'm delighted when imbecility has a stroke of inspiration.

Eliminate. Circumscribe. Condense to a natural necessity. Becoming is already accomplished.

She was nothing but expensive shoes, flowing rainbow-colored cloths.
Her slender body was her luxury.
When she tossed herself down on the white sheets, her lips were obsessively, obscenely thick.
She would speak for herself, her sleepy voice coming from bodily depths ravaged by desire.
She was so present that she was inapproachable.

Although he does not know her, Geoffroy de Rudel falls in love with the countess of Tripoli after hearing tales about her from the pilgrims returning from Antioch; he composes several songs in her honor, then joins the crusade so that he can see her; but on board the ship, he is afflicted by an illness so serious that everyone thinks he is dead. They nonetheless manage to bear him to Tripoli, where he is left in an inn; immediately informed of his arrival, the countess rushes to kiss her unknown lover, who regains consciousness, thanks God for having preserved his days until this moment, then gives his last breath. The countess takes up the veil because of the pain that she feels from this.

Gaia—overflowing with heavy fertility.
Gaia—nourishment for death.

Hesitant, her young body is like an offering in rustling black cloths.
Enticing childhood.
Abysses of Woman.
Desiring death and her desire.

Langueur lourde de la Tamise.
Le soir a des cristaux d'argent.

La mort a son regard de blonde tubéreuse.

Je veux être antagoniste, rompre les attaches, n'en point former de nouvelles, n'être qu'un ailleurs, un injoignable. Passant flâneur des rues caoutchoutées.

Copenhague est sous la neige.

J'habite des obstacles.

Doux maléfices qui t'emprisonnent.
Ta dispersion te faisait disparaître.

Le jour se montre, révélant sa confusion, la mienne, celle des rues, des têtes, des objets qui m'entoureront. J'apprends d'irrécusable façon que je suis ici-bas accident de Dieu.

Blanc d'absinthe
De la jacinthe.

Où est ta foule d'inconnus des étés, putain frigide ?
Ne me touche pas, précède ou suis-moi, mais ne te mêle pas à moi ; sois pour toi-même si tu en es capable, dans ton invraisemblable luxe de Femme à la vie étouffée par l'argent sans provenance.
Venise est une pleureuse abandonnée.
Montre-toi, comme elle, rétive, son ardeur occultée dans ses zones inatteignables.

Heavy flowing languor of the Thames.
The evening has silver crystals.

Death has its tuberous blond look.

I want to be antagonistic, break off attachments, form new ones, be merely an elsewhere, an unreachable person. A passerby strolling rubbery streets.

Copenhagen is snowed in.

I dwell in obstacles.

Sweet evil spells that imprison you.
Your dispersion would make you vanish.

The day appears, revealing its confusion, mine, that of the streets, the faces, and the objects surrounding me. I learn that I am unquestionably an accident of God on this earth.

Absinthe whiteness
Of the hyacinth.

Where is your crowd of summer strangers, frigid whore?
Don't touch me; walk ahead of me or follow me, but don't mix with me; exist for yourself if you can, in your incredible luxury of a Woman whose life is smothered in money coming from nowhere.
Venice is an abandoned woman hired to weep.
Show yourself to be restive, like the town, its ardor concealed in unreachable zones.

Putain honnête — offre-moi ce qui t'est refusé : une cendre d'innocence.
Venise — l'endeuillée.

Peu à peu, ma mémoire l'égare.
Quels sont tes gestes d'aujourd'hui ? Ton visage ? Ton regard ? Dans quels lieux ? En quelles présences ? Quels sont tes déplacements ? Tes désirs ? Tes satisfactions ? Tes espoirs ?
Je ne suis plus toi.

Sono solo
sono solo
sono solo
E più niente

Je ne veux que des oiseaux vivants.

Grelottis de la fauvette.

Lenteur de l'allongement noir des sourcils.

Ta folie ne retrouvera plus cet équivalent que lui était la mienne.
Tu ne savais pas que notre complicité perverse s'inscrivait dans le temps en moments inégalables.

Si jeune et belle *après* la mort. Où nos âges vrais ? Où nos domaines d'éternelle enfance, d'éternelle ignorance ? Où nos vies ? Quand commencent-elles ? De quoi s'accompagnent-elles ? Quelles sont leurs directions, leurs aboutissements ? De quels noms nous nommons-nous ?
Indivisible intégrité.

Honest whore—offer me what is refused to you: an ash of innocence.
Venice—in mourning.

Little by little my memory misplaces her.
What gestures do you use today? Your face? Your eyes? Your whereabouts? In the company of whom? Where do you travel to? Your desires? Your satisfactions? Your hopes?
I am no longer you.

Sono solo
sono solo
sono solo
E più niente

I want only live birds.

The warbler's shivering jingle.

Eyelashes slowly being lengthened and blackened.

Your madness will no longer find the match that my madness was for it.
You were unaware that our perverse complicity was recorded, in Time, in matchless moments.

So young and beautiful *after* death. Where are our true ages? Where are our realms of eternal childhood, of eternal ignorance? Where are our lives? When do they begin? What accompanies them? What are their directions, their outcomes? What names do we give ourselves?
Indivisible integrity.

Macías, poète espagnol de l'érotisme, qu'on surnomme *l'Amoureux*, est tué à travers les barreaux de sa prison par le mari jaloux qui l'y avait fait enfermer.

Camões, vivant du pain que, par charité, lui octroient les moines de Lisbonne.

Épuisé, à l'hôpital qui l'a recueilli, il dit : *Seul le Portugal, satisfait de la gloire de ses armes, dédaigne celle des lettres et des arts.*

Mer — décors étrangers.

Ta force est de submerger, de réduire à jamais au glacis de l'inconnu.

Reine taciturne.

J'aime ce que, massive, liquide, ta matrice a roulé dans ton incessant dérangement, qui aboutit avec tes bêtes mortes sur l'ensommeillement des plages.

La pierre que je tiens dans ma main est cristallisation de la gamme entière des roses mêlés de luminosités d'or et de capsules d'argent.

Pierre confiée à ma seule main ; mais je devine qu'elle est occupée à mourir de ton abandon ; que, sans toi, bientôt elle ne sera plus que petite dureté terne — la vie t'appartient, Mer des trop grandes richesses.

Ligne continue noir et jaune — la chienne.

L'esprit doit se chercher dans sa liberté.

Naissance — achèvement d'un temps de repli.

Le petit garçon dit :

— Si nous étions tous des champignons ? Des champignons dans la mousse des forêts silencieuses. Si nous étions sans cette torture de la parole ?

Nul ne lui répond.

La forêt est loin. Si loin que le petit garçon ne l'a jamais vue — il l'imagine à sa façon et se trouve néanmoins champignon heureux.

The Spanish erotic poet Macías, nicknamed *The Great Lover*, is killed through the bars of his prison cell by the jealous husband who had got him locked up there.

Camões, surviving on the bread that the monks of Lisbon give him in charity.

Exhausted, he declares at the hospital that takes him in: *Only Portugal, so proud of the glory of its army, disdains that of arts and letters.*

Sea—foreign props.

Yours is the force of submerging, of reducing forever to the glaze of the unknown.

Taciturn queen.

I love the liquid mass your womb has rolled incessantly, coming and going, ultimately abandoning your dead beasts on the drowsy beaches.

The stone I hold in my hand has crystallized the whole gamut of pinks mixed with golden luminosities and silver capsules.

Stone entrusted to my hand alone; but I sense it is occupied with dying because you have left it behind; that without you, soon it will be nothing more than a small dull hardness—life belongs to you, Sea, with your overabundant wealth.

Continuous black and yellow line—the female dog.

The mind must seek itself within its freedom.

Birth—end of a withdrawal period.

The little boy asks:

—What if we were all mushrooms? Mushrooms in the moss of silent forests. What if we didn't have to suffer this torture of speaking?

No one answers him.

The forest is far. So far that the little boy has never seen it—he imagines it in his own way and nevertheless thinks of himself as a happy mushroom.

Londres à ton cou.

Une forme dans le lointain des jardins, courbée sur la terre avec des mouvements si lents qu'ils sont peut-être inconsistants ; dans les arbres disséminés, le glougloutis des tourterelles, de branche en branche perchées comme de gros fruits duveteux ; ici et là, le piaillement des moineaux voltigeurs ; le panneau laqué d'un ciel gris ; une douceur de convalescence.
Le crépuscule emmitouflé s'apprête à tirer ses rideaux.

— Laisse-moi ton corps — je n'en ai pas aux âmes — je ne vis que du plaisir de son trouble.

Ni vie ni mort — vie et mort ne sont plus qu'une même force de conquête dans l'enveloppe que nous fûmes, conscients ou non de notre mérite, de notre destinée, de ce qu'elle est chargée de provoquer au-delà d'elle-même.

Il est minuit, et l'on place, droit et ferme, le Cid sur le bon cheval Babiéca, avec les chausses noires et blanches qu'il portait d'habitude, avec le manteau semé de croix d'argent ; son écu flottait suspendu à son cou ; sur la tête il avait un casque de parchemin peint, qui paraissait de fer ; le reste de son corps était revêtu de l'armure entière, et Tisona était attachée à sa main droite. Ainsi le Cid est vainqueur même après sa mort parce que saint Jacques marcha devant lui.

Quel tremblement est le nôtre ?
Dans les bars bruyants de ta ville, je te racontais cette histoire que tu ne connaissais pas. Peu à peu, tes yeux étincelaient, s'approfondissait ton regard, sur ton visage un graduel sourire d'exigeante cruauté ; ton corps devenait tuerie, immolation, massacre ; ton corps devenait Sexe — démence du Sexe, départs, aveuglements, débauche connue et consentie du Sexe — je te racontais cette histoire dont tu savais qu'elle te ressemblait.

Je marcherai la nuit près de mon amant mort.

London at your neck.

In the distant gardens, a shape bent over the soil and making such slow movements that they are perhaps insubstantial; in the scattered trees, the gurgle-like cooing of turtle doves, perched like big downy pieces of fruit on branches; here and there, the cheeping of fluttering sparrows; the backdrop lacquered with gray sky; a convalescent mildness.
The muffled-up twilight is about to draw its curtains.

—Leave me your body—I don't have one here among the souls—I only live off the pleasure of its turmoil.

Neither life nor death—life and death are no longer anything but the same force of conquest in the envelope we once were, aware or not of our worth, our destiny, of what it is responsible for causing beyond itself.

> *It was midnight, and The Cid was firmly placed upright on his good horse Babieca, wearing his usual black and white hoses and with his coat spangled with silver crosses; his shield was dangling from his neck; on his head he bore a helmet of painted parchment that seemed to be iron; the rest of his body was entirely covered with armor, and he held Tizona in his right hand. In this way, The Cid was victorious even after his death because Saint James marched ahead of him.*

What is this trembling we feel?
In the noisy bars of your town, I was telling you a story you had never heard. Little by little, your eyes started to shine, your look deepened; a smile of exacting cruelty gradually appeared on your face; your body became slaughter, immolation, massacre; your body became Sex—Sexual madness, departures, bedazzlements, the debauchery experienced and consented to by Sex—I was telling you this story which, as you knew, resembled you.

> *I will walk at night near my dead lover.*

Rien ne réussit qui ne soit en dépendance de la fonction d'initiation.

Abandonné sur la table, le fruit dans lequel, en creux, se dessine l'empreinte de ses dents.

Le péché est pensée.

Avenir dévorant.

Je n'ai été pris qu'à tes altérations séduisant en moi ma passion de l'irréel, que ton général dédain comblait.
Tu ne saurais espérer nulle forme de bonheur dans la répétitivité de l'habituel.
Après l'avoir leurrée, impitoyablement Mammon sacrifie la fantaisie.
Nos régions étaient douces . . .

Il faut compter en solitudes additionnées.

Il y eut ce temps où Savonarole s'écriait, menaçant : « Fais pénitence, ô Venise, fais pénitence ! »
Je te laisse, étrangère dans ton luxe rutilant ; le monde nous escorte, *amore mio*, comment pourrais-tu l'oublier ?
Elle lance avec mépris sur le canapé son long gant noir.
Venise — infidèle.

*C'è una città di questo mondo
ma cosi bella, ma cosi strana . . .*

Elle eut soudainement conscience de sa puissance érotique en portant dans un métro, sous le regard des hommes, une fraise à ses lèvres.

Nothing succeeds unless it depends on the function of initiation.

Left on the table, the piece of fruit with her teeth marks.

Sin is thought.

All-consuming future.

I was taken in only by your distortions, which seduced my passion for unreality and fulfilled it by means of your overall haughtiness.
You cannot hope for any kind of happiness in the repetition of what usually happens.
After deceiving fantasy, Mammon pitilessly sacrifices it.
Our regions were mild . . .

One must count by adding solitudes to each other.

There was that period of time when Savonarola would cry out the threat: "Repent, O Venice, repent!"
Foreign woman in your gleaming luxury, I'm leaving you; the world escorts us, *amore mio*, how could you forget this?
She haughtily tosses her long black glove on the sofa.
Venice—the unfaithful.

> *C'è una città di questo mondo*
> *ma così bella, ma così strana . . .*

She suddenly became aware of her erotic power when she brought a strawberry to her lips as men were watching her in a subway car.

En dépit de l'heure cependant avancée, il faisait nuit encore. Je me levai de mon lit, la tête embrouillée de fatigue. Comme chaque matin, sans doute ma famille devait-elle m'attendre autour de la table garnie du petit déjeuner. Je n'avais pas faim, mais je savais que, attentive, ma mère m'obligerait à manger au moins une tartine avec mon café au lait. « Par ce temps d'hiver, disait-elle, je ne veux pas que tu sois dehors le ventre vide. » Elle quêtait du regard l'approbation de mon père dont, d'apparence immuablement convenable, le cadavre ancien était assis sur une chaise à haut dossier décoré de clous d'or. Je descendis l'escalier. Ne s'y répandait pas l'odeur légèrement amère du café chaud. Dans la petite salle à manger, contrairement aux habitudes, ma mère avait tiré sa chaise auprès de celle de mon père, et ne bougeait pas davantage que lui. Instantanément, je compris avec soulagement que j'étais libre de déjeuner ou non, à ma convenance.

Contribuer à la constitution des silences, pourvu que, toutefois, ils aient le sens d'un flot de paroles.
Anonyme, le silence n'est que vide de mort.

Peu de femmes aiment l'exubérance ; moins encore lorsque, se prolongeant, elle les atteint.

Détails magiques.
Détails divins.
Détails défiant toute interprétation.
(Je me penche sur le tourbillon des inexplicables.)

Chargée d'elle-même, parfaitement libre, lisse, sans aspérité aucune, d'une froideur de vernis, mais des enflammements d'une telle condensation que, face à la brusquerie de leur violence, l'esprit est emporté par un vertige de désarroi.
Aigle cadenassé. Luminosité aveuglée. Cavité. Gouffre.
De qui espères-tu une main secourable ?

Despite the late morning hour, it was still dark outside. I got up from my bed, my mind muddled with weariness. Like every morning, my family was probably sitting at the table set for breakfast and waiting for me. I wasn't hungry, but I knew my attentive mother would make me eat at least one piece of toast with my café au lait. "In this winter weather," she would say, "I don't want you to be outside on an empty stomach." She searched my father's eyes for approval; with his invariable respectable look, the old corpse was sitting on a chair whose high back was decorated with golden studs. I came down the stairs. No slightly bitter smell of hot coffee in the air. In the small dining room, my mother had strangely dragged her chair next to my father's and was moving no more than he was. I instantly understood, with relief, that I was free to have breakfast or not, as I wished.

Contribute to putting kinds of silence together, provided, however, that they have the meaning of a flow of words.
Anonymous, silence is merely empty of death.

Few women like exuberance; even less so when it keeps going on and affects them.

Magic details.
Divine details.
Details defying any interpretation.
(I bend over the whirlwind of unexplainable things.)

In charge of herself alone, perfectly free, smooth, without the slightest rough spot, cold like varnish, but prone to such condensed flare-ups that the mind, faced with the abruptness of their violence, is swept away by a dizzying feeling of helplessness.
Padlocked eagle. Blinded luminosity. Cavity. Chasm.
From whom do you expect a helpful hand?

D'où la certitude d'une vie éternelle ?

Continuité cohérente.

Ma possible direction est un composé d'un indéfinissable nombre précédent.

Elle n'est ni innovante ni achevée, mais *poursuivante*.

J'agis dans ce qui est agi.

Somme des possibles qui sont en moi. (Soleil liquide blanchissant l'épaisseur grise du ciel.) Je ne m'utilise qu'au cent millionième. (Il faut rapporter du bois pour la cheminée.) D'une certaine manière, ces noms célèbres qui illustrent notre monde, ces éclats furent parcelles de moi-même. (Les deux chiennes somnolent à peu de distance de moi sur le canapé qui leur est consacré.) Le long calcul d'un crime *intelligent*. (Je bois à petites gorgées un café au lait brûlant.) Violence déchirante des tueurs fous, volontairement inconscients. (La vieille chaise semble pencher en avant.) Les tourbillons du jeu. (Autour de nous, les objets transformés en vie décorative — mais quand, où, comment s'exprime leur malignité ?) Amoureux éperdu des femmes. (En cette matinée de fin d'hiver, le silence, autant qu'il se peut former dans une infinité de brisures agressives.) Fasciné par le fin savoir érotique des femmes, leur incessante inventivité. (Les pierres des murs nous environnant sont à l'image de mes irrégularités.)

Je me façonne en me réduisant en cendres.

Je n'ai pas connu la non-anxiété d'être.

Expression verbale — forte organisation d'oubli.

Ta folie — supérieure.

Illusoires sont les ratures.

Where does the certainty of an eternal life come from?
Coherent continuity.
My possible direction is a compound of an indefinable preceding number.
The direction is neither innovative nor carried out, but rather *pursuing*.
I take action in what is acted on.

Sum of the possibilities in me. (Liquid sun whitening the gray thickness of the sky.) I use only a hundred-millionth of myself. (Wood needs to be brought inside for the hearth.) In a certain sense, those famous names that give color to our world, those sparkles, were parts of myself. (The two dogs are sleeping near me on the sofa reserved for them.) The long calculation of an *intelligent* crime. (I am sipping a burning hot café au lait.) Heartrending violence of insane killers, willingly unconscious. (The old chair seems to lean forward.) The whirl of the game. (Around us, objects have been transformed into decorative life—but when, where, and how is their malice expressed?) Lover distraught with women. (In this end-winter morning: silence, as much as it can take shape among an infinite number of aggressive kinds of cracking.) Fascinated by the fine erotic knowledge of women, their ceaseless inventiveness. (The stones in the walls surrounding us are the mirror image of my irregularities.)
I fashion myself by reducing myself to ash.

I have not experienced the non-anxiety of being.

Verbal expression—tightly organized oblivion.

Your—superior—insanity.

Crossing something out is illusory.

Il y a ignorance des habitudes —
nous n'habitons plus le même pays
nous ne parlons plus le même langage
les mêmes mots n'ont plus le même sens —
ta nudité parée de l'embrouillement vaporeux des linges raffinés s'est usée dans une première approche.
Nous sommes destins consumés.

Reviens une fois encore, la dernière sans doute, avec tes angéliques envoûtements, tes sourires, tes rires nocturnes de l'autre Occident ; reviens avec tes apparences d'enfant soumise qui s'est elle-même corrompue. Reviens, éteins-toi à jamais.

Hors de la terre printanière — sabres verts juvéniles des plantes nouvelles.

Geste — qui nous exprime, nous défend.

L'eau fraîche coule en cascades sur nos corps.

Force d'un esprit est distance.

Ruisselante, je t'aperçois de loin à ce carrefour où nous devions nous retrouver. Tu n'es qu'une tache mouvante dans l'épaisse grisaille de l'air. Un autobus passe. Tes cheveux en mèches sur le visage ; rapprochée de moi, tu me souris avec une expression déconfite. Tu me dis en anglais une phrase que je ne comprends pas. Cette légende védique où Indra envoie sur terre une pluie régénératrice qui a le pouvoir de faire pousser les herbes et de ressusciter les corps.
Pluie — sperme d'immortalité.

Habits have been forgotten—
we no longer live in the same country
we no longer speak the same language
the same words no longer have the same meaning—
the effects of your nudity adorned with refined, vaporously vague fabrics wore off during your first approach.
We are burned-out destinies.

Come back one more time, probably for the last time, with your angelic bewitchments, your grins, your nightly giggles from the other West; come back with those looks of a subjected child who has corrupted herself. Come back, put out your fire forever.

Above the spring soil—juvenile green swords of the new plants.

Gesture—what expresses us, defends us.

The fresh water cascades down our bodies.

A mind's force is distance.

I see you dripping with rain at that faraway intersection where we're supposed to meet. You're a mere moving mark in the thick gray weather. A bus goes by. The bangs of your hair have fallen down over your face; as you come closer, you smile, crestfallen. You say something in English I don't understand. That Vedic legend in which Indra sends to the earth a regenerating rain empowered to make grass grow and resuscitate bodies.
Rain—sperm of immortality.

Je me découvris conçu pour l'exactitude du vrai.

La petite fille observe à la jumelle dans les arbres le grand froissis d'oiseaux.

Cri de Properce :

Cynthia, qu'as-tu fait de ta raison ?

Jambes de femmes en mouvement.
Accumulation de silhouettes fines, réglées, construites sur une répétitivité de courbes.
Arrangement de futilités.
Parfums disséminés.
Regards qui n'en sont pas.
Effacements, éloignement.
En chacune d'elles, réminiscences qui édifient des séries de mondes ambigus.
(Ce jour-là — quel jour ? — tu étais vêtue d'un tailleur gris dont l'étroitesse dessinait abusivement ton corps ; la mousse de tes cheveux ramenés en chignon sur ta nuque ; ce jour-là, tu portais du linge blanc festonné de dentelles.)

Né à ce monde pour croiser quels autres destins ? —
pour délivrer
élever
éclairer
combler
encombrer
qui ?
Né à ce monde à peine pour moi-même.

I discovered I was conceived for the exactness of the truth.

With a pair of binoculars, the little girl watches the birds rustling in the trees.

Propertius's cry:

Cynthia, have you lost your mind?

Women's legs moving.
Accumulated slender silhouettes built and regulated according to repetitive curves.
Futilities arranged.
Perfume scents strewn about.
Looks that are not looks.
Women fading out, fading away.
In each of them, reminiscence constructs sequences of ambiguous worlds.
(That day—which day?—you were wearing a tight gray suit excessively outlining the shape of your body; your mossy hair was gathered into a chignon on the back of your neck; that day, you were wearing white clothing festooned with lace.)

Born into this world in order to meet up with what other destinies?—
in order to free
raise
elucidate
fulfill
obstruct
whom?
Born into this world barely for myself.

Il n'y a pas de retours.

J'identifie pour me défaire.

Je ne suis pas acceptation, mais crise angoissée.

Je veux cette jeunesse récalcitrante.

Nous devenions complices en étant contraires.
Nous assemblait un même goût inné du suicide.
Une même révolte, indéfinie, mais forte.
Un saccage du vrai présent au profit d'une vaste, simple et complexe rêverie de possessions despotiques.
Nous avions des âmes de doux équarrisseurs.
Le monde était notre domaine réservé.
Nous eussions pu vivre de la haine des conquêtes.
De nos multiples fragmentations.
De notre inflexible déloyauté.
De notre rare obscénité.
Nous étions convergence — puis fûmes ce repliement.
Inaccomplis, les faits ne laissent après eux que brûlure.

Qu'est-ce que l'homme ?
L'esclave de la mort, un voyageur passager
hôte de sa demeure . . .
Comment l'homme est-il placé ?
Comme une lanterne exposée au vent.
Qu'est-ce que la liberté de l'homme ?
L'innocence.

There are no returns.

I identify in order to undo myself.

I am not acceptance, but anxiety-ridden crisis.

I want this recalcitrant youthfulness.

We became accomplices while being opposites.
We were brought together by the same innate liking for suicide.
The same vague, yet strong revolt.
A ransacking of the genuine present in favor of a vast, simple, and complex reverie of despotic possession.
We had souls of mild-mannered slaughterhouse knackers.
The world was our private domain.
We could have lived off the hatred of conquests.
Off our multiple fragmentations.
Off our inflexible disloyalty.
Off our rare obscenity.
We were convergence—then were this withdrawal.
Unaccomplished, the facts leave only burns after them.

> *What is man?*
> *The slave of death, a passing traveler*
> *a mere guest of his abode . . .*
> *How is man positioned?*
> *Like a lantern facing the wind.*
> *What is man's freedom?*
> *Innocence.*

Pourquoi ne me parles-tu pas ? Pourquoi ne m'adresses-tu pas la parole ? Te suis-je à ce point étrangère ? N'avons-nous rien partagé au long de ces années d'existence commune ? N'aurions-nous été que deux froides, irréconciliables solitudes ? J'ai cependant vécu de toi, toi de moi, ne fût-ce que le temps que nous accordait le temps ; mais cela ne s'appelait-il pas rencontre ? Penser l'un pour l'autre. Concevoir l'un et l'autre. Se distinguer de l'autre afin de s'y conformer autant qu'il se peut envisager. N'avons-nous pas été recherche dirigée l'un vers l'autre ? Inconnus se révélant ? Intimité, pudeur de l'intimité s'abolissant ? N'avons-nous pas été vérité des corps liés ? Un mot, un seul . . .

— Oubli.

Matin de clarté lustrale
Jour hésitant dans ses grenadiers de lumière
Je suis debout — seul — devant des perspectives d'immensités vertes, sombres, violines, bleues
profondément terrestre
Revenu de ma mort
Moi renouvelé
Main large, prenante, regard en plongée vers mes indécisions
Je sais que m'attend une Femme
Je connais la couleur tempête de ma vie.

Polyphème s'interroge :
— Qui aimera ma laideur ?

Polyphème s'étonne :
— Quel est ce don de création qui m'a réduit à quelques droites ?

Ton nom n'est point Lydia, je le sais de reste ; mais, comme elle, tu es femme ; si même mon nom n'est point Horace, avec lui, d'une seule voix je m'emporte :

Why aren't you speaking to me? Why have you stopped speaking to me? Am I such a stranger to you? Haven't we shared anything during all these years of living together? Have we perhaps been only two cold, irreconcilable solitudes? Yet I have lived off you, and you off me, if only during this time granted to us by Time. But wasn't that called encounter? Each of us thinking for the other. Each conceiving the other. Each distinguishing him- or herself from the other in order to conform to the other as much as could be imagined. Haven't we been a quest in which each seeks the other? Strangers making themselves known to each other? Intimacy, the modesty of intimacy canceling itself out? Haven't we been the truth of linked bodies? One word, a single word . . .

—Oblivion.

Clear lustral morning.
Daylight hesitant in its pomegranate trees of light
I stand—alone—facing perspectives of green, dark, deep violet, blue immensities
deeply terrestrial
Back from my own death
Myself—renewed
Big grasping hand, a look downward toward my indecisiveness.
I know a Woman awaits me
I know the stormy color of my life.

Polyphemus wonders:
—Who will love my ugliness?

Polyphemus is surprised:
—What is this gift of creation that has reduced me to a few straight lines?

Your name is not Lydia at all; I know all too well what it is; but you are a woman like her; even if my name is not Horace, I lose my temper with a single voice:

> *Cum tu, Lydia, Telephi* . . . Ah ! Lydia cesse de louer devant moi Télèphe au cou de rose, Télèphe au bras d'ivoire ! Je sens alors la colère gronder dans mon cœur ; mon esprit se trouble ; *Uror, seu tibi candidos* . . . Ô ! douleur ! quand je vois tes blanches épaules honteusement meurtries par lui *sive puer furens Impressit memorem dente labris notam* . . .

Toujours elle semble surgir d'une impossibilité, un peu essoufflée, un peu ébouriffée, pressée, nerveuse, un peu étourdie.

Elle arrive pour accorder sa présence, pour être un moment de beauté gratuitement concédée.

Elle est petite au milieu des gens aux aguets ; elle redoute d'être en retard, néanmoins sachant qu'elle a calculé son temps afin de ne pas risquer un manquement ; ponctualité qui fait partie de sa conscience.

Elle est aussitôt souriante, caressante, livrée avant d'être sollicitée.

Malgré sa foule, un peu terne, la gare londonienne n'est guère bruyante . . .

La durée nous diminue en possibles.

Me regarder n'est pas l'objet —
l'objet étant de ne plus m'apercevoir, en aucune façon, sous nulle forme, dans aucun langage, fût-il de gémissements de douleur
l'objet est de me renier au plus tôt
insondable
contraire
ennemi
l'objet est l'objet lui-même, c'est-à-dire, en définitive, *erreur*.

Lenteur ouateuse de sa langue.

Polyphème dit :
— Ce regard, que je ne puis poser sur moi.

> *Cum tu, Lydia, Telephi* . . . O Lydia, when you commend Telephus' rosy neck, and the waxen arms of Telephus, alas! my inflamed liver swells with bile difficult to be repressed. Then neither is my mind firm; *uror, seu tibi candidos* . . . I am on fire, whether quarrels rendered immoderate by wine have stained your fair shoulders sive puer furens Impressit memorem dente labris notam . . .

She always seems to be emerging from something impossible, a little out of breath, a little disheveled, in a hurry, nervous, a little scatterbrained.

She arrives in order to make a gift of her presence, in order to be a moment of beauty given away freely.

She is small among people ever on the lookout; she fears being late though she knows she has calculated how long it will take to avoid the risk of not fulfilling her duties; punctuality belongs to her conscience.

She immediately smiles, is affectionate, giving herself over to others before they make demands on her.

Despite the rather dull crowd, the London train station is hardly noisy . . .

Duration diminishes our possibilities.

To gaze at me is not the point—
the point is not to perceive me any more, in any way, in any shape, in any language, even in painful groans
the point is to deny me as soon as possible
unfathomable
adverse
enemy
the point is the point itself; that is, ultimately, *error*.

Her tongue's cottony slowness.

Polyphemus says:
—That gaze, which I cannot aim at myself.

Italie — désespérée
des abandons
des tragédies
des faux calculs
du mépris.
Je marche sur ta terre immémoriale.

Venise de la fuite.
Elle était mince forme jaune, lèvres crispantes, conçue pour les dévastations.

Je ne me suis jamais senti vivre que dans l'amour, disait le fragile Leopardi. *Pourtant tout le reste du monde alors pour moi comme s'il était mort.*

Je ne suis que dans le rêve face à un moi-même adoptant ma profonde conformité.

J'aime la douce tentation du divin.

Soie verte.

La nuit dernière, quelqu'un a marché dans la longue allée sablée du jardin.
Les corps se démultiplient au gré de leurs désirs.
Peut-être, pour cette visiteuse, la matinée d'autrefois était-elle encore claire, silencieuse, comme elle le fut à cet instant fugace de sa jeunesse.
Te rappelles-tu la beauté foisonnante des fleurs nacrées des magnolias ?
Et que, ce matin-là, tu avais, sans le vouloir, atteint l'impressionnante beauté de l'assurance heureuse ?

Italy—desperate
because of relinquishments
tragedies
false calculations
contempt.
I walk on your immemorial earth.

Venice of escape.
Conceived for devastations, she was slim and yellow-shaped, with irritating lips.

I have never felt myself live except when I am in love, said fragile Leopardi. *Yet in that state, the rest of the world is as if it were dead for me.*

Only in dreams am I faced with a myself taking on what most deeply conforms to me.

I love the sweet temptation of the divine.

Green silk.

Last night, someone strolled down the long sandy path of the garden.
Bodies divide into other bodies in accordance with their desires.
Perhaps for that visitor, the morning back then was still as clear and silent as she herself was at that fleeting moment of her youth.
Do you recall the lush beauty of pearly magnolia flowers?
And that, the same morning, you had unwillingly attained the impressive beauty of cheerful self-confidence?

Je recherche mon nom dans de si anciennes colonnes d'écriture que faible est ma chance de réussir un jour à me nommer.

Contentez-vous donc des syllabes de mon invention que je vous fournis pour favoriser votre distinction d'entre le nombre.

Je ne me suis pas souhaité — une forme me définit ailleurs.

— Tu as froid ?
— Un peu.
— Serre-toi contre moi.
— C'est en toi qu'il faudrait que je puisse me glisser.
— Glisse-toi en moi.
— M'y autorises-tu ?
— J'aime les doubles.

Je suis soudainement ce que tu souhaitais —
départ
défi
insolite
injure
violence
sang
le monde autour de moi est à sacrifier à l'unique plaisir, sans prétexte, sans excuse ni remords.

Soudainement, je suis parcelle de ta volonté.

J'aimais l'une de tes culottes, d'un jaune soufre, à la large échancrure, qui laissait dans tes déplacements entr'apercevoir ton sexe.

Petite feuille d'arbuste séchée, aux teintes marbrées de bois verni.

Y demeure encore la ferme puissance du vaisseau central et, comme diluée, celle des veinules adjacentes — qui furent à cette menue forme sang de la vie.

Ne s'y est soustrait qu'un essentiel — flexibilité, mouvement.

I seek my name in such old handwritten lists that my chances of one day finding a name for myself are slim.

So content yourselves with the invented syllables with which I provide you in order to enhance your distinction among the numbers.

I did not wish myself to be—a form defines me elsewhere.

—Are you cold?
—A little.
—Snuggle up next to me.
—It's inside you that I'd need to slip.
—Slip inside me.
—Will you allow me to do so?
—I like doubles.

I am suddenly what you were wishing for—
departure
challenge
out of the ordinary
insult
violence
blood
the world around me is to be sacrificed uniquely to pleasure, without pretexts, excuses, remorse.

Suddenly, I am a part of your willpower.

I loved one of your panties. It was sulfurous yellow and large on both sides of the crotch so that whenever you walked your sex could be glimpsed.

This withered little shrub leaf, mottled with varnished-wood-like hues.

The persistent powerful firmness of both the central vein and the seemingly diluted adjacent venules—which represented the lifeblood of this tiny form.

Only one essential aspect is missing—flexibility, movement.

L'instant n'est, dans sa valeur et sa complexité, qu'indicible.
De la sorte, investi du caractère du Mystère.
Ce qui le compose nous admet en nous refusant.
Nous ne sommes pas partie de lui-même, mais accidents parallèles.
Nous nous bornons au rôle d'hôtes conviés dont il est convenu qu'on ignorera l'identité.
L'instant nous laisse à nous-même — dans notre indigence réfléchissante.
L'instant nous déserte.
Nous ne pouvons de lui saisir que de faibles vibrations, que le temps métamorphose en pâle trace de mémoire.
Nous n'appartenons qu'en figurants à la composition du présent.
Nous sommes voués à la négation du temps.

Avec de lourds bateaux rouquins
Venus des brumes hollandaises
Le port usé dans des matins
Couleur de glaise
Cargaison de poissons salés
Et de marins aux barbes vertes
Revenus que pour s'en aller
Dans ma chambre fenêtre ouverte
Je voyais Londres de ma chaise

Jeu de vie — qui effectue
Jeu de vie — qui engendre
Jeu de vie — qui produit
Jeu de vie — qui crée
Extraire du rien n'était que calcul logique — seul exécutable.

Grâce réceptive qui nous ouvre à la dimension transcendantale de l'Univers
Herbe — je suis Herbe
Arbre — je suis Arbre
Ciel — je suis Ciel

In its value and complexity, a moment is ultimately inexpressible.

In this way, endowed with the character of Mystery.

What it consists of admits us while rejecting us.

We are not part of it, but rather parallel accidents.

We restrict ourselves to the role of invited guests whose identities, by agreement, will remain unknown.

A moment leaves us to ourselves—in our mirror-like destitution.

A moment deserts us.

We can grasp only weak vibrations of a moment, which time metamorphoses into pale traces of memory.

We belong to the makeup of the present only as walk-on roles.

We are doomed to be negated by time.

With heavy red-haired ships
Hailing from hazy Holland
The harbor is worn out in the mornings
A clayish sludge color
Cargos of salted fish
And green-bearded sailors
Come back home only to sail back out
At the open window of my room
I was sitting on my chair and watching London

Life game—that performs
Life game—that begets
Life game—that produces
Life game—that creates

Extracting from nothingness was merely a logical calculation—the only feasible one.

Receptive grace that opens us up to the transcendental dimension of the Universe

Grass—I am Grass
Tree—I am Tree
Sky—I am Sky

Immensité — je suis Immensité
Eternité — je suis Eternité
Dieu — je suis Dieu.

Pour t'accepter toute, il eût fallu me perdre, ou me reconstituer selon l'image d'anciens vouloirs en moi ; devenir ton aventure sans but autre que celui du moment présent, de ta triste fantaisie destructrice, de ta redoutable capacité à être.
Tu es vouée aux abandons.

Où étaient tes amours — sinon moi ?
Dans quels ensevelissements — sinon les tiens ?
Qui protégeais-tu — sinon ton infernale séduction ?
À quoi te destinais-tu — sinon à la vie souterraine ?
Qui eût pu t'aimer — sinon moi ?

Tu me faisais parcourir Londres avec l'enthousiasme de ta jeunesse. À une marchande installée au coin d'une rue, tu achetas une jacinthe, dont tu voulais orner une petite table de ta chambre. J'aurais voulu t'expliquer que cette fleur est l'emblème de la douleur ; qu'exilé du Ciel, Apollon gardait les troupeaux du roi Admète. Malheureux d'amour, le frère de Diane rechercha l'amitié. Le jeune Hyacinthe devint son compagnon. Un jour qu'ils jouaient ensemble au palet, jaloux de la préférence qu'il accordait à Apollon, Zéphyr souffla puissamment le disque sur la tête du jeune homme, qui tomba mort. Inconsolable, Apollon, qui avait ce don, changea son ami en fleur, appelée *Jacinthe*.
Ce matin-là, Londres avait des couteaux dans ses rues.

Tu m'attachais par l'extrême restriction volontaire du cercle de tes idées. Tu m'attachais d'être, de ne savoir être que toi, à l'exclusion de toute autre évasion — vocation de chair axée sur l'attraction du Sexe et ses enjolivements pervers.

Immensity—I am Immensity
Eternity—I am Eternity
God—I am God.

In order to accept you completely, I would have needed to lose myself, or put myself back together by using the images of former desires inside me; to become your adventure with no other goals than those of the present moment, your sad destructive fantasy, and your formidable ability to exist.

You are doomed to being abandoned.

Where were your lovers—other than me?
In what burial shrouds—other than yours?
Whom were you protecting—other than your infernal seductiveness?
What were you destining yourself for—other than the underground life?
Who could have loved you—other than me?

With your youthful enthusiasm, you had me running all over London. From a street-corner flower merchant, you bought a hyacinth with which you wanted to decorate a small table in your room. I wanted to explain that the hyacinth symbolizes grief; that when Apollo was banished from heaven, he would keep watch over King Admetus's herd. Diana's lovesick brother was seeking friendship. Young Hyacinth became his companion. One day as they were throwing the discus, Zephyr—who was jealous of Hyacinth's greater love for Apollo—powerfully blew the discus down on the head of the young man and killed him. Inconsolable, Apollo, who had the gift of changing people into flowers, transformed his friend into the flower called *Hyacinth*.

That morning, the London streets brandished knives.

You bound me by means of the intentionally and greatly restricted circle of your ideas. You bound me so that I would be, would know how to be, only you, excluding all other escapes—a carnal calling centered on the attractions of Sex and its perverse embellishments.

Je n'avais connu que toi capable de s'installer n'importe où dans le monde et d'aussitôt y creuser une sorte de cuve aspirante d'où rien ne pouvait provenir qui fût différent de ton obsession.

J'ai pris de toi ce qu'on en pouvait prendre : les feux noirs du diabolisme ; mais en homme avisé.

J'ai pris de toi des phases de ton ombre, sans en rien m'entamer.

Elle n'était que perpétuelle agitation, perpétuel mensonge, perpétuel obstacle, perpétuelle réparation, perpétuelle tentation —
elle était abolition de la mort
de l'idée de la mort
par la rapidité de son impatience
le foudroiement de ses envies
la distance de sa folie.
Elle était *l'innommable* sans enfance.

Sans heures, sans lieux sont les nuits des amours.

L'enfoncement de toi fut-il cette proximité de mer, ton corps dérangeant la vieille ville italienne ?

Comme le meurtre, l'amour de chair s'exécute dans le *rien*.

Italie — froide —
des secrets de famille
des pauvretés déguisées
des orgueils blessés
des insurmontables impossibilités
des désertions féminines
des angoisses religieuses
des interdictions du hasard
des sombres et grandioses personnages.
Italie manquante — et royale
que les mers dorlotent.

You were the only person I had known who was capable of settling anywhere in the world and immediately digging a sort of cistern pump from which nothing could flow that was different from your obsession.

I took from you what could be taken: the black fires of devilry; but as a sensible man.

I took from you phases of your shadow, without slicing anything out of myself at all.

She was nothing but perpetual agitation, perpetual lying, perpetual obstruction, perpetual atonement, perpetual temptation—
she was the abolition of death
of the idea of death
through her lively impatience
her lightning-quick cravings
her distant madness.
She was the *unnamable* without a childhood.

The nights of love are timeless, spaceless.

Was the nearby sea thrusting into you, your body upsetting the old Italian town?

Like murder, carnal love functions in *nothingness*.

Italy—cold—
family secrets
masked poverties
wounded prides
insurmountable impossibilities
feminine desertions
religious anguishes
random prohibitions
dark grandiose personalities
Italy lacking—and royal
pampered by the seas.

T'approchant, chaque fois je me suis, souriant, souvenu du proverbe grec : « Il n'est pas permis à tout le monde d'aborder à Corinthe. »

Mais généreuses, gratuites sont les maligneries de ton corps ; tu n'es pas Laïs — je m'en réjouis.

À la *scuola Ricetti*, les enfants chantent :

> *Grazia di primavera*
> *piuma di poesia*
> *più bianca, più leggera*
> *del fior della gaggia*

Donne-moi ta main.

Il faut, Cérinthe, avoir, hélas, un cœur de fer pour rester à la ville (Tibulle).

Elle allume une cigarette, dont le bout est aussitôt grenaillé de son rouge à lèvres.
Londres s'encotonne.

Tout n'est que *perspective d'écriture*.

Où est le point commun de ce qui n'est que division ?
L'espacement.

Folie à la conquête du bonheur, mais engagée sur des domaines d'anéantissement.

Polyphème pense :
— Quel est mon maître ?

Whenever approaching you, I always smiled to myself as I recalled the Greek proverb: "Not everyone is allowed to go to Corinth."

But you give away your body's malice freely, generously; you're not Lais—and I'm delighted you're not.

At the Scuola Ricetti, the children sing:

> *Grazia di primavera*
> *piuma di poesia*
> *più bianca, più leggera*
> *del fior della gaggia*

Give me your hand.

Alas, you need a heart of iron, Cerinthus, to remain in the city. (Tibullus).

She lights a cigarette, whose other end is immediately spangled by her red lipstick.

London becomes cottony.

Everything is but a *perspective of writing*.

What does something that consists only of division have in common? The spaces between.

Crazy about conquering happiness, but venturing into the realms of annihilation.

Polyphemus wonders:
—Which one is my master?

Io
ma mélancolique des prés.

La vie ne nous concerne immodérément qu'au moment de son épuisement.
Tentatrice, sachant ne plus pouvoir être saisie.
Habile à faire regretter ce qu'elle n'a laissé qu'entrevoir.
L'irréel la pare somptueusement — puis elle s'évanouit.
L'imaginer nue, indéfectible comme le temps ?
Vivre la Mort de la Vie.

Beauté noble de sa sévérité d'expression.

Ce mot dérisoirement douloureux et naïf :
— Je brûle mon carnet d'adresses, et je te suis où tu veux.

Je sais qui n'est plus moi.

Car rien n'est plus sot qu'un sot rire (Catulle).

Aujourd'hui, sixième jour du printemps. Il neige.
J'ai eu peur de ma vie à dix-sept ou vingt ans.
Vieil homme, j'ai peur de ma mort.

Commerce de Martial, le malicieux :

> *Vis te, Sexte, coli : volebam amare.*
> *Parendum est tibi ; quod jubes, coleris :*
> *Sed si te colo, Sexte, non amabo.*

> *Vous voulez que je vous honore, Sextus : moi, je voulais vous aimer. Il faut vous obéir, et, puisque vous le voulez on vous honorera. Mais si je vous honore, Sextus, je ne vous aimerai plus.*

Io
my melancholic of the meadows.

Life immoderately concerns us only when it is running out.
A temptress knowing how to avoid being taken hold of any more.
Skillful at making us regret what she has let us only glimpse.
Unreality adorns her sumptuously—then she vanishes.
Imagine her naked, indestructible—like Time?
Experience the Death of Life.

The noble beauty of her severe look.

This laughably desperate, naïve message:
—I am burning my address book and will follow you wherever you wish.

I know who is no longer myself.

There's nothing sillier than a silly laugh (Catullus).

Today, the sixth day of spring. It's snowing.
At seventeen or twenty, I was afraid of my life.
Now an old man, I'm afraid of my death.

In the company of Martial the malicious:

> *Vis, te, Sexte, coli: volebam amare.*
> *Parendum est tibi; quod jubes, coleris:*
> *Sed sit e colo, Sexte, non amabo.*
>
> You want me to honor you, Sextus; as for me, I wanted to love you. I must obey you and, because you wish to be honored, you will be. But if I honor you, Sextus, I will no longer love you.

Embrasse-moi.
(Sur la place majestueuse de la grande ville, le soleil est éblouissant.)
Plus tard, seuls sur un banc public, tu t'étendras de tout ton long sur mes genoux.
Je te parle d'une autre femme. Tu m'écoutes. Tu es jalouse.
(Victor Hugo logea dans l'une de ces austères demeures.)
Embrasse-moi.

Nous te haïssons, te méprisons ; je te hais, te méprise, moi que tu t'es choisi comme confesseur.
Fais l'amour humblement, ventre lacéré.
Quitte ta superbe, comme tu te départirais d'un masque.
À Venise l'impudique, ce soir s'achève la fête.

Puissance d'obscénité par laquelle l'esprit d'abord s'échauffe, puis s'obstrue.
(Je te laissais à ton corps.)

Réveillée, la chienne reste longtemps pensive, une patte pendante hors de son coussin. Il semblerait qu'elle doive impérativement comprendre ce qui lui a été annoncé dans son sommeil, qu'elle éprouve une certaine difficulté à accommoder les images retenues du rêve, à les organiser de cohérente façon.
Attendrissante dans son incompréhension.

Qui suis-je parallèlement au temps ?
Ma musique ?
Mon empreinte ?
Mon souffle ?
Ma dissolution ? — il se peut.
Ombre, je me convoque.
(Croix contradictoire d'Apulée. *Alterutrae.*)
Je me confonds dans un bien qui m'a été accordé et me façonne dans un mal que j'ai connu — le Juge est clémence.

Kiss me.
(On the majestic square of the big city, the sunlight is dazzling.)
Later, when we're sitting alone on a bench, you'll stretch out over my knees.
I speak to you about another woman. You listen. You're jealous.
(Victor Hugo lived in one of these austere mansions.)
Kiss me.

We hate you, scorn you; I hate you, scorn you, I—your chosen confessor.
Make love humbly, your belly slashed.
Cast off your haughty air as you would remove a mask.
In shameless Venice, this is the last night of the Carnival.

Obscene power with which the mind warms up, then gets obstructed.
(I left you to your body.)

Awakened, the dog long remains pensive, one paw dangling over its cushion. She seems bent on understanding what was announced to her during her sleep, but is struggling to make sense of the images recalled from the dream and to organize them coherently.
Her incomprehension is touching.

Who am I as a parallel to Time?
My music?
The tracks I leave?
My breath?
My dissolution?—perhaps.
Shade, I summon myself.
(Apuleius's contradictory cross. *Alterutrae*.)
I blend myself into a good granted to me and fashion myself into an evil I experienced—the Judge is clemency.

M'astreindre à aligner ma vie de chaque jour sur le matériel d'objets qui m'entoure, me sert, me divertit, m'émerveille ; mon regard peut à l'instant être bouquet de minuscules fleurs séchées dans un vase d'argent, s'attarder sur une collection de dés à coudre, dont la faïence décorée est à l'œil plaisante ; voir sous la vitre le tableau qui, comme tous ses semblables, se défait pour se recomposer chaque jour lui-même, si ce n'est pas à chaque moment ; me complaire, au loin, à la contemplation d'une petite série d'aquarelles aux couleurs vives ayant le son de la joie ; méditer sur un christ de bois doré fiché sur son velours grenat dans l'encadrement découpé à l'image d'un corps d'église ; pénétrer la rumeur dentelée d'une plante que le jour fortifie devant une fenêtre — tant de choses pour plaire, séduire, que des hasards guidés offrirent à ma vue . . .

Être œil est attirer l'inamovible, exhaler des influx de vie à ce qui pourrait n'être que somnolence retirée.

Ce nervosisme joyeux, cette souveraine insouciance, cette habileté exercée à la séduction, ces abandons inattendus à la lassitude d'enfant, ces larmes aussitôt rentrées, cette science des corps, cette innocence encore réelle, cette passion du risque, ces soudaines et insurmontables impuissances, ces désespoirs désordonnés, cette jeunesse en quête du monde.

À Londres, les nuits sont violettes.

Au dernier versant de l'été, la forêt est chaude, grosse comme pourrait l'être une femme proche d'allaiter, lourde, difficile, enchevêtrée, réticente ; mais imprégnée d'images anciennes de chasses, d'ignominies, de morts immotivées, de sacrifices dénués de sens ; sereine, mais chargée de secrets, prête à désorienter, à faire trébucher, à griffer au sang, à tordre les membres ; raideur inviolable, ultime refuge.

Je souhaiterais que tu fusses dans ta profondeur chevelue ma demeure dernière, à l'abri de toute curiosité.

Forêt des enfouissements — source des réveils.

Toits mauves des maisons sous la bruine.

Compelling myself to put my daily life in line with the material objects surrounding me is useful, amusing, and fills me with wonder. I can just now look at a bouquet of tiny dried flowers in a silver vase; linger over a collection of thimbles whose decorated glaze delights the eye; study below a glass pane the painting which, like all paintings, comes apart only to put itself back together every day, indeed in every moment; take pleasure from afar in contemplating a little series of bright watercolors that create a joyful sound; meditate on a gilded wooden statue of Christ stuck on a garnet-colored piece of velvet in a frame cut out to resemble a church; penetrate the dentate murmuring of a plant in front of a window and fortified by daylight—so many things that please and seduce, that guided random chance enabled me to see . . .

To be an eye is to attract the irremovable, to breathe out the impulses of life toward what can only be withdrawn somnolence.

This joyous nervousness, this sovereign heedlessness, this skill applied to seduction, these unexpected relinquishments to childlike lassitude, these immediately withdrawn tears, this science of the body, this still-genuine innocence, this passion for risk-taking, these sudden and unsurpassable fits of helplessness, these moments of disorderly despair, this youthfulness in quest of the world.

In London, the nights are violet.

On the last slope of summer, the forest is warm, bloated as a woman might be when about to breastfeed—sultry, difficult, entangled, reticent; but impregnated with ancient visions of hunts, ignominious acts, senseless sacrifices; serene, but laden with secrets, ready to lead you astray, to make you stumble, to scratch you till you bleed, to twist your limbs; inviolable stiffness, ultimate refuge.

I would like you—your hairy depths—to be my last abode, sheltered from all curiosity.

Forest of burials—source of awakenings.

Mauve house roofs in the drizzle.

Peindre — s'aveugler pour voir.

Solitude froide et attirante de la pierre noire.

Œil-Oiseau. Œil-Fleur. Œil-Ciel. Œil-Herbe. Œil-Arbre. Œil-Lumière. Œil-Blés. Œil-Fruits. Œil-Sourire. Œil-Silhouette. Œil-Femmes. Œil-Silence. Œil-Connivence. Œil-Questionnaire. Œil-Découverte. Œil-Invective. Œil-Combinaison. Œil-Équation. Œil-Démultiplication. Œil-Appel. Œil-Dieu. Œil-Accident. Œil-Œil. Je me propose à ma propre méditation. Rien. Occasionnel. Tournoiement d'un absurde. De quoi ai-je rêvé ? Jeune. Très jeune. D'une absence indéfiniment présente. De me faire autre. Forme provisoire. Une heure. Une nuit. Œil-Univers. Œil-Perfection. Œil-Immortalité. Œil-Anonymat. Je n'ai emprunté jamais que les routes interdites. Atteindre un quelconque but à la fin du périple n'avait pour moi nulle signification. Œil-Évanouissement. Œil-Vastitude. Œil-non-Regard. Œil-Abréviation.
J'étais l'envers de la règle instituée. Page raturée. L'incartade.

To be alive — is — Power —

Marche à ta mesure ; bénis qui tu es.
Or, les fils de Dieu vinrent un jour se présenter devant l'Éternel, et Satan vint aussi au milieu d'eux. L'Éternel dit à Satan : D'où viens-tu ? Et Satan répondit à L'Éternel : De parcourir la terre et de m'y promener. L'Éternel dit à Satan : As-tu remarqué mon serviteur Job ? Il n'y a personne comme lui sur la terre ; c'est un homme intègre et droit, craignant Dieu, et se détournant du mal. Et Satan répondit à l'Éternel : Est-ce d'une manière désintéressée que Job craint Dieu ?

Fille de Cadmus.

— Qui meurt ici ?
— Moi — nous tous.

Painting—blinding yourself in order to see.

Cold alluring solitude of the black stone.

Eye-Bird. Eye-Flower. Eye-Sky. Eye-Grass. Eye-Tree. Eye-Light. Eye-Wheat Stalks. Eye-Fruit. Eye-Smile. Eye-Silhouette. Eye-Women. Eye-Silence. Eye-Connivance. Eye-Questionnaire. Eye-Discovery. Eye-Invective. Eye-Combination. Eye-Equation. Eye-Multiplication. Eye-Appeal. Eye-God. Eye-Accident. Eye-Eye. I offer myself up to my own meditation. Nothing. Occasional. The whirling of something absurd. What have I dreamt? Young. Very young. Of a forever present absence. Of making myself into someone else. A temporary form. One hour. One night. Eye-Universe. Eye-Perfection. Eye-Immortality. Eye-Anonymity. I've always taken only prohibited roads. To attain some goal at the end of the voyage had no meaning for me. Eye-Fainting Fit. Eye-Vastness. Eye-Non-Looking. Eye-Abbreviation.

I was the reverse side of the instituted rule. A crossed-out page. A prank.

To be alive—is Power—

Walk to your own measure; bless who you are.

Now there was a day when the sons of God came to present themselves before the Lord, and Satan came also among them. And the Lord said unto Satan, Whence comest thou? The Satan answered the Lord, and said, From going to and fro in the earth, and from walking up and down in it. And the Lord said unto Satan, Hast thou considered my servant Job, that there is not like him in the earth, a perfect and an upright man, one that feareth God, and escheweth evil? Then Satan answered the Lord, and said, Doth Job fear God for nought?

Daughter of Cadmus.

—Who is dying here?
—Me—all of us.

Noyade du ciel.

Ce qu'on aime protéger.

Libellule, de *libellulus*, diminutif de *liber*, livre, parce que, prétend-on, ces insectes tiennent leurs ailes au contact comme les feuilles d'un livre — mais cette étymologie est incertaine.
Plus connues sous le nom populaire de *demoiselles*, elles sont caractérisées par des ailes presque égales en longueur, à réseau très compliqué. Leurs yeux énormes, occupant la plus grande partie de la tête, ont une belle couleur brillante, vert doré ou bleue.
Leurs amours se décident par un enlèvement.

Polyphème est affecté. Un oracle lui a prédit qu'il serait un jour privé de lumière par un ennemi sans merci.
— Aussi dois-je m'accoutumer à voir en moi-même, murmure-t-il.

Froide Venise dans la solitude de son vrai visage.
J'y suis le passant endolori au bras de la Femme longuement désirée, comme somnolente dans ses folles richesses, sa méconnaissance des vérités du réel.
Beauté haute.
Beauté lente.
Beauté de verrerie.
Cette nuit, dans le grand palais aux cent portes, tu seras nue comme Venise.

Volonté opposée.

Mer — laine mousseuse.

The sky is drowning.

What we love to protect.

    Dragonfly, *libellule*, from *libellulus*, the diminutive of *liber*, book, because these insects supposedly keep their wings together like the pages of a book—but this etymology is dubious.
    Better known by the popular name of *demoiselles*, dragonflies are characterized by wings nearly equal in length, with very intricate lacework. Their enormous eyes, which take up the greatest part of their heads, have beautiful shiny blue or golden green colors.
    Love is settled by an abduction.

    Polyphemus is uneasy. An oracle has predicted he will one day be deprived of light by a ruthless enemy's act.
    —So I must get used to seeing inside myself, he murmurs.

    Cold Venice in the solitude of its true face.
    I am the aching passerby on the arm of the long-desired Woman who seems drowsy in her insane riches, in her ignorance of the truths of reality.
    High beauty.
    Slow beauty.
    Glasswork beauty.
    Tonight, you will be naked like Venice in the great palace with its hundred doors.

Willpower in conflict.

Sea—foamy wool.

Je ne prétends ni à m'égaler ni à me désidentiner ; ni à me fuir ni à me surplomber. Je ne prétends à être qu'un inconcevable se souhaitant des rencontres, des haltes communes ; s'alignant sur le degré qui l'éclairera. Voilà une région où les Femmes sont adroites. Je me porte donc à elles avec simplicité, à la façon d'un enfant bien dressé. La compagnie est trop inexplicablement charmeuse ; mais le vide, le profond noir qui s'ensuit ? À qui, après tout, l'attribuer ? À ma méconnaissance, certes ; je ne suis que pensée, volonté d'œuvre...

Enfant, Polyphème se demande :
— Que dois-je apprendre du monde des cyclopes ?
De la paume, il aveugle son œil.

Crimen relinquit vitae, mortem qui appetit (Syrus).

Ce qui, impuissant, est en nous attente.

Ferme doucement les yeux. La chambre est d'une immobilité de velours. (Connais-tu le beau nom grec de la coccinelle — *kokkos* ?)

Dix cloches sonnent dans l'air métallique du matin ; peut-être ne sont-elles que cinq, trois ; peut-être n'y en a-t-il qu'une — qu'importe ; j'entends la Joie, la Plénitude d'Être, l'Étonnement de vivre, dérangement de la placidité ; j'entends la Réalité des Âmes.
Le coq chante aussi, par ici, dans un coin proche derrière des arbres et les premières maisons ; il se peut qu'à sa façon il ne se chante pas que lui-même ; tout est en accord à un certain degré d'invisibilité.
Le mulot trottine sur le petit mur pour s'épargner le danger des regards ; il connaît les règles de son milieu.
La limace rousse s'est immobilisée dans la touffe d'herbe rencontrée au cours de sa cauchemardesque propulsion ; ne pas autour d'elle faire trembler la terre ; il se peut qu'elle soit occupée à se considérer en qualité de parfaite vulnérabilité.

I claim neither to equal myself nor to strip myself of my identity; nor to flee from myself, nor to loom over myself. I claim to be only an unconceivable person who seeks encounters, common halts; situating himself at the level that will enlighten him. This is a region where Women are deft. I thus go to them unaffectedly, like a well-behaved child. Their company is too inexplicably charming; yet what about the emptiness, the deep darkness that ensues? To whom, after all, should it be imputed? To my ignorance, of course; all I am is thought, a will to create . . .

When he was a child, Polyphemus wonders:
—What must I learn from the world of Cyclopses?
With the palm of his hand, he blinds himself in one eye.

Crimen relinquit vitae, mortem qui appetit (Syrus).

What, inside us, is infertile expectation.

Close your eyes softly. The room is motionless like felt. (Do you know the beautiful Greek name for the lady bug—*kokkos*?)

Ten bells toll in the metallic morning air; perhaps there are only five or three; perhaps only one—what does it matter? I hear Joy, Plenitude of Being, Astonishment at being alive, perturbation of placidness; I hear the Reality of Souls.

The rooster also crows here, in a nearby spot behind some trees and the first houses; it could be that, in its own way, it crows out more than itself alone; everything is harmonized at a certain degree of invisibility.

The field mouse scampers along the low wall in order to save itself from the danger of being spotted; it knows the rules of its environment.

The russet slug is immobilized by the tuft of grass it encountered during its nightmarish propulsion; don't make the ground shake around it; it could be busy pondering its perfect vulnerability.

Un oiseau, un bruit, une porte qui se ferme, une voix qui appelle — ensemble familier qui n'est rien que parce que je m'y trouve provisoirement incorporé —
mais où est MOI ?
J'ai le sentiment heureux de ma pesanteur et de mon volume affirmés dans la dentelle fraîche du matin d'été.

Oiseaux picorant craintivement le grain sous la pluie.

Équilibre de la Terre — notre vie.

Par centaines, beautés des fleurs qui se préparent à leur somptueux éclatement.

Légèreté — soupir de l'esprit.

Seul éclat de moquerie — s'ouvrent les fêlures.

Nous, passagers. *Donne à celui qui demande, et ne te détourne pas de celui qui veut emprunter de toi* (Mt., V, 42).
Je vis la peur de l'autre, ou ne suis pas.

Les enfants sont altérés.

Mer — ensevelissante
nu, je me présente à la vapeur de tes cristaux.

Beauté lénifiante de ton approche —
Mer constante.

A bird, a noise, a closing door, a voice calling out—a familiar grouping that exists only because I find myself temporarily included in it—
but where is ME?
I have the happy feeling that my weight and my volume have been asserted in the lacy coolness of the summer morning.

Birds timidly pecking at grain in the rain.

Equilibrium of the Earth—our life.

Hundreds of flowery beauties readying to burst into sumptuous bloom.

Lightness—a mind sighing.

A mere mocking burst—the cracks open.

We are voyagers. *Give to him that asketh thee, and from him that would borrow of thee turn not thou away.* (Matthew 5:42).
Either I experience another man's fear, or I do not exist.

The children have been altered.

Sea—enshrouding
naked, I introduce myself to the haze of your crystals.

Soothing beauty of your approach—
Steady sea.

Ne reste d'elle à ma mémoire que des *actions* ; point de paroles.
Ainsi s'exprimait-elle — s'apportant elle-même dans les circonvolutions de l'existence.

Maisons de sel.

Notre heureuse terre chaude.

Visage insoutenablement angélique dans la salle de concert tandis que l'orchestre interprète les bienséantes détresses de Schubert.
Sa main glacée, figée dans le creux de la robe lamée.
Après le concert, elle s'endort d'un coup dans la voiture, comme un enfant.

Vénus change Adonis en anémone rouge. *Elle répand sur le sang du jeune homme un nectar embaumé*, dit Ovide.

Robe noire au tissu lourd.
Plantée dans la nuit sur le quai désert de la gare.
Les trains passaient dans leur fracassement métallique.
Les lumières étaient jaunes et brusques.
Quel signe était-elle ainsi chargée d'incarner ?

Je t'ai laissée sur le balcon d'une chambre d'hôtel de province, te faisant dans la rue signe de la main en m'éloignant, pressé que j'étais, non pas de rejoindre la direction que tu croyais, mais une différente — je prenais le soir même un train pour Copenhague, où une autre femme elle aussi m'attendrait avec angoisse sur le balcon de sa maison.
Tu avais ta robe rouge à laquelle manquait toujours un bouton.

Sol invictus.

Only her *acts* remain in my memory; not her words.
This is how she expressed herself—bearing herself away into the circumvolutions of existence.

Salt houses.

Our warm happy earth.

Unbearably angelic face in the concert hall while the orchestra interprets Schubert's seemly distress.
Her icy hand, which she keeps stuck in the crotch of her lamé dress.
After the concert, she drops off to sleep in the car, like a child.

Venus changes Adonis into a red anemone. *She pours fragrant nectar,* says Ovid, *over the young man's blood.*

Thick black dress.
She was standing there in the night on the deserted platform.
The trains clanged and squealed by.
The lights were yellow and harsh.
What sign was she supposed to embody?

I left you on the balcony of the provincial hotel room, waving to you from the street as I hurried away, though not to take the direction you imagined but rather a different one—that same evening I took a train to Copenhagen, where another woman would also await me anxiously on the balcony of her house.
You were wearing your red dress on which a button was always missing.

Sol invictus.

Sa voix d'enfant joyeuse — Satan s'accorde des langueurs.

Voici l'âge de ta ressemblance...

Coup de fouet vert de la mer.
Rêve de tous les abandons.
Sentiment de tous les luxes du corps.
Possibilité de toutes les ambitions sans nécessaires accomplissements.
Démarche aux limites de l'inconnu.
Accueil et refus.
Générosité et orgueil.
Je suis l'homme de passage, dépouillé de son nom, de la pesanteur de ses anciens regards.
Lent assoupissement en moi de l'étranger.

Pâles instants où se forment des chapelets de négations comparables à des emmêlements de riens.
(Peut-être l'esprit a-t-il subtilement quitté ses faisceaux de nervures incitatrices ; peut-être le temps s'essaie-t-il à des basculements ?)
Je pourrais écrire des lignes de mots sans suite — mais, curieusement, je suis plus attiré par les prénoms ; sans doute en raison de leur sonorité, car le sens musicien ne m'a pas quitté ; la vie rayonnante de l'ouïe, le tissage de ses profondeurs. Probablement, le préférable est-il de passer outre ?

Vents poilus.

Café sombre dans cette rue étroite proche du petit théâtre.
Ta joliesse d'adolescente me saccageait le cœur.
J'ai été sur le point de te demander de partir sur-le-champ au hasard avec moi.
Nous aurions passé notre première nuit dans n'importe quel train en partance pour n'importe quelle lointaine ville étrangère.
Ton visage avait l'aura bouleversante de l'enfance.

Her joyous childlike voice—Satan lets himself have some languor.

Now the age of your resemblance has come . . .

The sea's green whiplash.
A dream of all the ways of letting go.
A feeling of all the body's luxuries.
The possibility of pursuing all the ambitions without necessarily fulfilling them.
Taking steps at the limits of the unknown.
Welcome and rejection.
Generosity and pride.
I am the passerby, stripped of his name and the gravity of his former gazes.
Inside me the foreigner is slowly drowsing off.

Pale moments when rosaries of negations comparable to tangles of trifles are formed.
(Has the mind perhaps subtly fled its fascicules of instigator nerves; is time perhaps having a go at upheavals?)
I could write down lines of words without consequence—but, strangely, I am more attracted by first names; probably because of their sonority, for a musician's sensitivity has never left me; the radiant life of hearing, its woven depths. Isn't it probably better to carry on regardless?

Hairy winds.

Dark café in this narrow street near the little theater.
Your adolescent cuteness was ravaging my heart.
I was on the brink of asking you on the spot to leave with me for a random destination.
We would have spent our first night in a train departing for some faraway foreign city.
Your face had the deeply moving aura of childhood.

J'étais devant toi force et incapacité.
Tu me disais que tu étais fiancée...
(Je regardais au-dessus du comptoir un savant travail d'ouvrier ébéniste.)

Je mourrai l'esprit plein d'herbages roux et verts.

Je fabrique ce qui a génialement été fabriqué.

Le chant provient d'une direction de la dimension intérieure de l'interprète, de sa capacité d'appropriation des séries de motifs sensibles ; il se peut que, chez certains d'entre eux, intervienne leur réflexion ; mais, immanquablement, elle se limitera à leurs seuls points supérieurs, les plus apparents — car, avant tout, le chant doit être *continuité*.

Cuivre mat du chandelier à Sept branches
Jours de la semaine
Langues de feu
Jour des Lumières
Degrés célestes
Pétales de la Rose
Arbre cosmique
Pater Noster
Vie éternelle
Perfection

Maman, apporte-nous la Flamme chaude
Nos yeux ont tant besoin de clarté

Certaines rues de Londres ont ta démarche, tes sourires, tes agacements, tes incompréhensions, tes bouderies, tes emportements, tes pensées cachées — certaines rues de Londres ont l'exquise et amère saveur de l'inaccompli.

Facing you, I was force and inability.
You told me you were engaged . . .
(I was looking at some highly skilled woodwork above the bar counter.)

I will die with my mind full of green and russet grasses.

I make what has been made with genius.

The song comes from one direction of the singer's inner dimension, from his or her capacity to appropriate several series of sensitive motifs; some singers perhaps let their mind intervene; however, without fail, their thinking will be restricted only to the superior, most obvious qualities of the motifs—for, above all, singing must be *continuity*.

Dull copper of the Seven-branched candelabra.
Days of the week
Tongues of fire
Feast-day of Lights
Celestial steps
Petals of the Rose
Cosmic Tree
Pater Noster
Eternal Life
Perfection

> *Mother, bring the warm Flame to us*
> *Our eyes are in such need of clarity*

Some London streets possess your gait, your smiles, your irritations, your moments of incomprehension, your fits of pouting or anger, your hidden thoughts—some London streets have the exquisite bitter taste of unfulfillment.

Tu m'attirais non confondue, exceptionnelle, unique, imprévisible, capable de disparaître sous prétexte qu'on t'attendait, subitement surgie où, croyait-on, tu ne pouvais te trouver, exhumant de quelque cachette de toi des flots de pétales de roses que tu jetais dans la rue comme un poème se fût soudain composé ; rieuse, dominatrice, disposant seule de la présente seconde, à nul soumise, déchirure de liberté, désinvolture de la provocation, occupée exclusivement de tes désirs, pesante d'expansion et de mort, légère de ton caprice.

Arrêtée dans la rue devant une boutique de vêtements féminins. Envieuse. En elle-même tremblante. Soudain ramenée aux douloureux et angoissants émerveillements des impatiences de l'enfance. Une roseur instantanée au visage. Une brillance nouvelle dans le regard. Un imperceptible piétinement sur place. Un élan contenu du corps vers la possible réussite du désir. L'émoi de la possession qui, en une fraction de temps, pourrait devenir réalité, contentement de l'espérance — transfiguration.

Mer —
sur la plage nue
ouverte
jeune présence léchée par la mort des vagues
que seule une violence ranimerait.

— La nuit est-elle régénération ? se demande Polyphème, angoissé.

Amplitude, largesse — chargé de pluie le jour nouveau se plisse contre la vitre ; bientôt le temps d'enfouir les graines en terre, de préparer la munificence des semaines chaudes au ciel de mince voilerie ; matins ébouriffés d'oiseaux, tiède fraîcheur, enveloppante épaisseur des verdures d'arbres, limitant les distances, circonscrivant les percées du regard ; l'âme a des émois simples, des versements d'infini ; tout est racine de Terre ; les voix anciennes murmurent :

I was attracted to your unmistakable, exceptional, unique, unpredictable qualities. You were capable of vanishing with the excuse that someone was waiting for you, then of suddenly popping up in a spot where no one thought you could be, unearthing from one of your hiding places a flow of rose petals that you would toss over the street as if a poem had suddenly been composed; cheerful, domineering, alone possessing the present moment, subjected to no one, a shred of freedom, with an offhand provocative manner, exclusively occupied with your desires, weighty with expansiveness and death, light in your whimsicality.

Stopping in the street in front of a women's clothing shop. Envious. Inner trembling. Suddenly taken back to the painful and anxiety-ridden marvels of childhood impatience. Instantaneously blushing. A new shine in her eyes. An imperceptible stamping of her feet. Her body withholding its drive to make desire possibly come true. Emotion at the idea of possession which, in a fraction of a second, could become reality, the satisfaction of hope—transfiguration.

Sea—
on the open-ended
naked beach
a young presence licked by the death of the waves
could be brought back to life only through some kind of violence.

—Is night regeneration? wonders Polyphemus, feeling anxiety.

Magnitude, generosity—the early morning, with its pouring rain, creases up against the window; soon the time will come to bury seeds in the soil, to make ready for munificent warm weeks under a thinly veiled sky; mornings tousled by birds, lukewarm yet refreshing, the enveloping thick foliage of trees, limiting distances, circumscribing what the eyes sharply perceive; the soul has simple emotions, deposits of infinity; everything is a root of the Earth; the ancient voices murmur:

Annua venerunt Cerealis tempora sacri ;
Secubat in vacuo sola puella toro.

Le royaume des Terres se sacralise.

Le chemin au-dessus de —
cette transparence redoutablement attirante, mortelle de
Mer
une inattention serait une telle étincelle de vouloir, un mol affadissement, une fragmentation de défaillance
acceptée
chute rapide
poids de l'enfoncement liquide
ne pourrait-on point être tentation, effort aisé vers l'oubli
il faut se raidir
se reculer
ne plus consentir à l'étrangeté de l'affinité
se reformer dans ce qui est concrétion de matière
suivre le chemin, bordure préservatrice
alignement, but
marcher avec bonheur sur ses jambes souples
continuer à aller
poursuivre
s'écarter
Mer — matricielle.

S'inscrire dans le *plus nettement*. Se propose en conséquence une décortication intérieure de l'être, pour l'essentiel réduit à des dimensions lilliputiennes ; ses hoquets d'émotion n'ayant plus valeur que de curiosité, car les profondeurs n'y sont point exprimées ; ce que, peut-être, nous eussions néanmoins penché à admettre autrement avec une exigence plus relâchée.
(Illustrer de gravures à l'eau-forte.)

Gémissant, Polyphème répète :
— *Orco*, l'Ogre.

Annua venerunt Cerealis tempora sacri;
Secubat in vacuo sola puella toro.

The realm of Lands makes itself sacred.

The path above—
this fearfully attractive, mortal transparency of
Sea
a heedless step would be such a spark of willingness, a dulled feebleness, a fragmentation of failure
  accepted
  quick drop
  weight of sinking into liquid
  couldn't one be temptation, an easy effort toward oblivion
  one needs to stiffen
  to stand back
  to consent no more to the strangeness of affinity
  to change one's ways inside what is concretion of matter
  to follow the path, protective border,
  alignment, goal
  to walk contentedly on flexible legs
  to continue to go forward
  to pursue
  to step away from
  Sea—matrix-like.

Put your name down within what is the *most distinct*. You are consequently offered an inner stripping of your being, essentially reduced to Lilliputian dimensions; its emotional outpourings worth no more than curiosities, since no depths are expressed; which we would perhaps have nonetheless been inclined to accept otherwise, with more relaxed demands.
(Illustrate this with etchings.)

Groaning, Polyphemus repeats:
—*Orco*, the Ogre . . .

La mince jeune femme brune aux lèvres fortement maquillées de rouge noir m'emmenait je ne savais où, convaincu que j'étais d'être enlevé enfin comme, au secret de moi-même, je le souhaitais chaque soir ; soustrait miraculeusement à une première organisation de mon destin, dont je ressentais la certitude qu'il ne devait pas être le mien.

Nous suivions des rues dans une ville agitée ; le parfum de la jeune femme me semblait être quelque chose de préhensible auquel je pourrais éventuellement me raccrocher si, par accident, elle venait à me perdre.

Nous marchions longtemps ; l'une après l'autre, les rues se succédaient ; ma mémoire n'en retenait que des images de murs gris, sales, parfois maculés d'affiches déchirées, d'inscriptions blanches que je ne savais pas lire.

Nous arrivions dans une grande maison sombre, accueillis par des femmes comme des fruits secs enrobées dans de longues robes noires.

Il y avait une petite fille trop blonde, à la figure livide, fine.

Avant de tomber de fatigue dans un lit enflé d'un édredon rose, je n'avais à constater que ma déception pour la continuité immuable d'un destin cependant refusé.

Dans l'obscurité du petit balcon, forme secrètement mouvante, elle quitte un à un ses vêtements.

Nudité proche.

Étourdissante présence du nu.

Gélification de l'émoi.

Elle est cette impudence à demi dissimulée par la nuit.

Debout, livrée, audacieuse, frêle d'hésitation.

Elle est combat muet entre abandon et réticence.

Silhouette trop blanche.

Prête à tous les feux destructeurs.

Malgré sa jeunesse extrême, un passé à tout jamais la prive des clartés de l'innocence.

Elle est du côté des ténèbres.

Mer — lèvre.

La vague effleure la courbure sombre du sein.

I had no idea where the slender brunette, her lips smeared with black-red lipstick, was leading me off to. I was convinced that I had at last been abducted as, in my innermost being, I had hoped to be every evening; that I had been miraculously removed from the initial organization of my destiny which, so I was certain, should not be mine.

We were heading down streets in a busy city; the young woman's perfume seemed to be something tangible to which I could perhaps cling if, by chance, she lost track of me.

We had been walking for a long time; street after street went by; my memory was retaining only the dirty gray walls, sometimes stained with shreds of posters and with white graffiti I could not read.

We arrived at a big dark house and were ushered in by women who were like pieces of dry fruit enrobed in long black gowns.

A small, too blond girl with a pale slim face was standing there.

Before I fell exhausted into a bed swollen with a pink eiderdown, all I had to ponder was my disappointment at the unchanging continuity of a destiny that I had, however, rejected.

In the nocturnal darkness of a small balcony, a secretly moving shape strips off her clothing piece by piece.

Nearby nakedness.

Deafening presence of nudity.

Gelled emotion.

She is shamelessness half-hidden by the night.

Standing there as if handed over, at once bold and frail in her hesitation.

She wages a speechless battle between shyness and letting herself go.

Too white a silhouette.

Ready for all the destructive blazes.

Despite her tender age, her past forever deprives her of the clarities of innocence.

She belongs to the shadowy side.

Sea—lip.

The wave just touches the dark curve of the breast.

J'attends de moi d'être celui
qui serait non pas une nouveauté aux étendues inconnues de moi, mais reflet inattendu.

Mon désir alors était de l'apprendre avant qu'elle ne fût à tout consentante, la précédant de mon expérience.

De la découvrir se vêtant à ses couleurs, touchante parfois de maladresse, de non-savoir.

Elle avait l'âge encore des remontrances, mais je l'inféodais par mes silences.

Fraîcheur matinale des rues presque désertes.
(Je souhaite m'égarer dans l'oubli.)

Aube, retour au regard diversifié du jour — toutes choses sont à présent dénombrables.

Blés en masse serrée sur le coulant de la colline. Blés blancs, blés grisonnants en attente de la restitution lumineuse du Soleil.

Plus haut, sur le sommet, dans une indécision de la clarté, le Calvaire de pierre noire moussue.

Le matin large ouvert jettera dans un ciel de tenture idéale la fantaisie bariolée des cerfs-volants.

Courses et rires d'enfants.

La chaleur se fait épée verticale.

Éclatement rogue de midi.

La cloche sonne.

On rentre d'un pas fatigué sur les chemins sableux, traquant l'ombrage secourable.

Il y aura sur la table dressée la grosse carafe d'eau glacée au verre embué.

Boire ; se guérir par lampées de la brûlure sèche.

Nourritures fraîches dans les grands plats creux d'épaisse faïence blanche.

Temps mort du silence au fond des maisons protectrices.

I expect myself to be
him who would be not a novelty at the unknown limits of myself, but unexpected reflection.

I desired back then to teach her before she would consent to everything, putting my own experience first.

To discover her dressing in her own colors, and she was sometimes touching in her mistakes, her ignorance.

She was still at the age of remonstrance, but my silences gained her allegiance.

Morning coolness of nearly deserted streets.

(I want to go astray in oblivion.)

Dawn, the return to a diversified daytime gaze—all things are now countable.

Masses of wheat hugging the smooth slope of the hill. White wheat, graying wheat waiting for the luminous return of the Sun.

Higher up, at the summit, the mossy black stone Calvary in hesitant light.

The wide-open morning will cast the motley fantasy of kites up into an ideally drape-like sky.

Children racing around and laughing.

The heat turning itself into an upright sword.

The haughty explosion of high noon.

The church bell rings.

Wearily we go back over the sandy paths, hunting for helpful shade.

On the table set for lunch there will be a large misty pitcher of ice water.

To drink; to heal oneself by swigging the burning dryness.

Fresh food in big, thick, white earthenware plates.

A silent lull in the depths of protective houses.

Approche ta bouche, c'est ton plaisir, le mien ; tu es dévoreuse, moi dévoré, mais enfin je me relâche sur ta langue, dans ta gorge — et t'appartiens par ce qui, en moi, est pure Force.

Je lie à mes vies mes objets chers. De la sorte, par *imprégnation*, ils en adoptent la signification — le résultat.
Modeste, j'ai une tendresse pour de modestes objets, qui m'ont servi, me servent. Je ne me sens en rien leur *possesseur*. Je les respecte dans la circulation qu'ils ont à accomplir.
L'objet est vie — point de matière qui soit exempte de vibrations.
Beaux objets voués à la Beauté.
Il y a *rencontre*.

Mort — habillement de la raideur
Et ses répartitions de couleurs atténuées qui produisent une grandeur nouvelle
En serait-il ainsi de nous ? (Quelles pourraient être nos couleurs éternelles ?)
Qui eussent, en ce cas, échappé au pourrissement
car il y a, naturellement, menace d'absolue dissociation —
Qui, éventuellement, se charge de notre minutieuse protection ?
Il est probable que s'exerce l'impitoyable partition.

Polyphème pense :
— *Caeci sunt oculi, quum animus alias res agit.*

Offre ton cou de silex pur à la scintillance du bijou.

Thomas Chatterton se donne la mort après avoir souffert plusieurs jours de la faim. Il avait à peine dix-huit ans.
Promenons-nous ce matin dans Londres, l'air est vitrifié.
Edward Young voit, à cinquante ans, mourir son épouse et sa fille. Il écrit *Les Nuits*.
Promenons-nous ce matin dans Londres, la Tamise est pelissée.

Bring your mouth closer, it's your pleasure and mine; you're the devourer, I the devoured, but at the end I come on your tongue, in your throat—and belong to you by what, inside me, is pure Force.

I link my precious objects to my lives. In this way, by *impregnation*, they adopt the meaning of my lives—the result.

Being modest, I have a liking for modest objects that have been and still are useful to me. In no way do I feel I *own* them. I respect them as they move along the circuit they must follow.

Objects are life—not mere matter void of vibrations.

Beautiful objects devoted to Beauty.

An *encounter* takes place.

Death—outfit of stiffness
And its distribution of dimmed colors produces a new grandeur
Is it possibly the same with us? (What could our eternal colors be?)
Which would, in this case, have escaped rotting
for the threat of absolute dissociation naturally exists—
Who is perhaps responsible for our meticulous protection?
A merciless division probably occurs.

Polyphemus thinks:
—*Caeci sunt oculi, quum animus alias res agit.*

Offer your pure flint neck to the jewel's sparkle.

Thomas Chatterton kills himself after suffering from hunger for several days. He was barely eighteen years old.

Let's stroll in London this morning, the air is glassy.

At the age of fifty, Edward Young watches his wife and daughter die. He writes *Night Thoughts*.

Let's stroll in London this morning, the Thames is furry.

James Thomson arrive d'Écosse dans une telle misère qu'il est nu-pieds mais il a avec lui son premier poème, *L'Hiver*.

Promenons-nous ce matin dans Londres, les boutiques élégantes sont luisantes de cire.

Promenons-nous ce matin dans Londres, ta main est froide.

J'aspirais à m'envahir moi-même . . .

Nul ne peut se comparer à . . . Il n'est que des formations, des constitutions méthodiquement calculées afin qu'elles soient en capacité de faire intervenir l'opportun, le frottement — l'apparition de constitutions nouvelles prises des anciennes.

Le but consiste à obtenir la gymnastique mécanique de cette mêlée jamais inactive.

Pure beauté concise du contraste.

Quelqu'un — des hauteurs supérieures — contemple, attentif :

— Je fais en sorte, se dit-il à lui-même, que la règle ne soit pas transgressée.

De l'ombre proche se fait entendre une voix narquoise :

— Je fais en sorte que la transgression soit encore la règle.

Tes fautes étaient un jeu de Femme en voie d'accomplissement.

Je savais comment te ramener, te saisir, te garder —

corps

corps-feu

corps-glace

corps-scorpion

corps-meurtre

corps-sang

corps-sangsue

corps de la démesure

corps de la dévastation

corps-faim

corps-putain

corps que l'enfance n'a pas investi

corps-orage

James Thomson arrives from Scotland in such wretchedness that he is barefoot; but he has his first poem, "Winter," with him.

Let's stroll in London this morning, the elegant shops are shiny with wax.

Let's stroll in London this morning, your hand is cold.

I aspired to invade myself . . .

No one can compare himself to . . . Only formations exist, configurations methodically calculated so that timeliness and friction are brought in—the appearance of new configurations derived from former ones.

The goal is to obtain the gymnastic workings of this never inactive free-for-all.

Pure concise beauty of the contrast.

Someone—from the superior levels—attentively looks on:

—I act in such a way, he tells himself, that the rule will not be transgressed.

From a nearby shadow a sardonic voice makes itself heard:

—I act in such a way that transgression remains the rule.

Your faults were the childlike games of Woman in the process of ripening.

I knew how to bring you back, grasp you, keep you—
body
body-fire
body-ice
body-scorpion
body-murder
body-blood
body-leech
body of excessiveness
body of devastation
body-hunger
body-whore
body in which childhood was not vested
body-storm

corps-attachement
corps-avortement
corps-suicide.
(Dans quelles rues, à quels sexes de rencontre accordes-tu aujourd'hui ce corps-cadavre ?)

Immobilité dénudée où suffit une parole pour que se fracture le destin. Collusion folle et, sur-le-champ, nous devenions d'autres nous-mêmes. Rien ne fut dit qui, comme à l'ordinaire, ne pût être à tout instant inversé.

Mer — indifférente
trop d'espace, de profondeur, trop d'inconnu
Mer à survoler
noyeuse de ciel
à tes bords nos corps étendus sont sans réalité
main rampante dans l'humidité molle du sable
Mer — proche
tenace, fuyante, identique
mais précautionneuse sur le sein nu
Mer — mort.

Danses. Musiques. Chants. Danses. Musiques. Chants. Danses. Suicides.

Cliquetis de boucles d'oreilles.

Pouvoir de détruire est moins pouvoir que plaisir.

Accord secret d'inconnues tendresses.
(La rose dorée offerte hier a dans son vase un regard d'oiseau.)

body-attachment
body-abortion
body-suicide.
(In which streets, to which sexual organs encountered do you grant this body-corpse today?)

Stripped immobility in which a single word suffices to fracture fate.
Insane collusion and, on the spot, we became other we's.
Nothing was said which, as usual, could not be inverted at any moment.

Sea—indifferent
too much space, depth, too much that's unknown
Sea to fly over
Sea drowning the sky
at your edges our stretched-out bodies lack reality
hand groping in the limp wetness of the sand
Sea—nearby
stubborn, evasive, identical
yet cautious on the naked breast
Sea—death.

Dancing. Music. Singing. Dancing. Music. Singing. Dancing. Suicides.

Jingling earrings.

Power to destroy is less power than pleasure.

Secret harmony of unknown kinds of tenderness.
(In its vase, the golden rose offered yesterday is like a bird watching.)

Lève-toi, mon amie, ma belle, et viens !
Car voici, l'hiver est passé ;
La pluie a cessé, elle s'en est allée.
Les fleurs paraissent sur la terre,
Le temps de chanter est arrivé,
Et la voix de la tourterelle se fait entendre dans nos campagnes.
Le figuier embaume ses fruits,
Et les vignes en fleur exhalent leur parfum
Lève-toi, mon amie, ma belle, et viens !

Soirs où je te lisais ces versets du *Cantique des Cantiques*.
Tu étais claire, attentive, jambes croisées sur un gros coussin rouge.
Tes lèvres étaient pâles.
Tes yeux profondément noirs.
J'aimais la petitesse de tes mains.
La façon dont tu rejetais d'un coup de tête tes cheveux en arrière.
Ton front blanc soudain révélé comme une lumière.
Dans la blouse souple, tes seins étaient hauts et durs.
Parfois tes yeux se fermaient.
Ton visage devenait d'une imposante gravité.
Autour de nous le silence de la nuit.
Égoïste alliance de deux êtres.
Tu portais au cou un petit rubis.
Tache cramoisie sur ta peau rousse.
J'étais le gardien de la fragilité de l'entente.

> *Fais-moi voir ta figure*
> *Fais-moi entendre ta voix*
> *Car ta voix est douce, et ta figure agréable.*

Londres, animal soyeux.

Mer — aperçue
   brusque ouverture sans limites qui semble déverrouiller les oppressions terrestres
   inhumaine étendue qui répond à des désirs d'évasion de l'âme.
   Mer — idée d'aventure.

Rise up, my love, my fair one, and come away!
For, lo, the winter is past, the rain is over and gone;
The flowers appear on the earth;
The time of the singing of birds is come,
And the voice of the turtle is heard in our land;
The fig tree putteth forth her green figs
And the vines with the tender grape give a good smell.
Arise, my love, my fair one, and come away!

Evenings when I would read *The Song of Solomon* to you.
You were clear-minded, attentive, your legs crossed on a big red cushion.
Your lips were pale.
Your eyes deep black.
I loved your small hands.
The way you shook back your hair.
Your white forehead suddenly revealed as light.
In your loose blouse, your breasts were high and hard.
Sometimes your eyes closed.
Your face would take on an impressive seriousness.
Around us the silence of the night.
Egoistical alliance of two human beings.
You would be wearing a red ruby around your neck.
A crimson stain on your russet-colored skin.
I would watch over our fragile mutual understanding.

> *Let me see thy countenance,*
> *Let me hear thy voice*
> *For sweet is thy voice, and thy countenance is comely.*

London, silky animal.

Sea—glimpsed
sudden unlimited opening seemingly unbolting terrestrial oppression
inhuman expanse responding to the soul's desires to escape.
Sea—idea of adventure.

Entre nous — l'écart ; signe de liberté, d'indépendance ; signe heureux de possession décidée d'un commun accord ; point de resserrement mécanique, vulgaire ; point de liens à la lourdeur encombrante.

Désir et plaisir pouvaient alors se confondre dans une volontaire distance établie, évaluée par avance ; l'accointance ne laissait rien au hasard ; les corps en permanente volupté dans leur proche éloignement consenti.

De la sorte, nous étions le magnétisme des chambres closes où ni jour ni nuit n'avaient consistance ; de l'obscénité nous étions l'arc surtendu ; il ne s'agissait que de *renvoi*, de conscience électrifiée, de recomposition nerveuse de la Tentation des âges premiers — dans les parages, se tenait aux aguets Satan, quêteur d'âmes mais nos âmes, elles, ne perdaient rien de leur vigueur saine ; elles exerçaient avec *expérience*.

Monde ophidien.

Huit serpents à sonnette avaient été débarqués à Liverpool, venant d'Amérique. Un montreur d'animaux, nommé W. Manders, les acheta et les fit voir, à Northampton, dans une ménagerie. Au-dessous de la cage des serpents à sonnette était un récipient, que l'on entretenait plein d'eau chaude pour maintenir autour de ces animaux une douce température. L'eau étant venue à bouillir avec trop de violence, le gardien s'approcha un moment du foyer, pour arranger les tisons, et malheureusement il laissa la cage entrouverte. En revenant, il s'aperçut que l'un des huit serpents s'était échappé. En effet, le terrible crotale bondissait au milieu de la ménagerie, sifflait et dressait sa tête d'une façon menaçante. On essaya de capturer le fuyard, qui s'introduisit dans les cages d'autres animaux, mordant au naseau un énorme buffle. À une voiture était attelé un magnifique cheval de haras. Le serpent s'élança sur lui et le mordit. Aussitôt, le cheval se mit à ruer, à se cabrer avec tant de violence qu'il parvint à faire tomber le reptile qu'il broya sous ses fers ; mais peu d'instants après avoir été mordu, il fut saisi de tremblements. Ses yeux sortaient de ses orbites, et il faisait entendre des hennissements plaintifs. Quelques minutes après, il expirait dans une effrayante agonie.

Que voulais-tu mordre de ta langue fourchue — serpente de tous les charmes ?

Between us—the gap; a sign of freedom, independence; a happy sign of possession decided upon by mutual agreement; no vulgar automatic coming closer together; no burdensome heavy bonds.

Desire and pleasure could thereafter blend at a distance willingly established and evaluated beforehand; being linked left nothing to chance; two permanently voluptuous bodies at the slight distance that they had agreed to keep from each other.

In this way, we were the magnetism of closed bedrooms in which neither day nor night had any substance; we were the overly taut bow of obscenity; only *give and take* mattered, maintaining an electrified awareness, a nervous reconstitution of the Temptation of the first ages of mankind—Satan, the collector of souls, was standing on the lookout in the vicinity; but as for our souls, they lost nothing of their healthy vigor; they were functioning with *experience*.

Ophidian world.

Eight rattlesnakes from America had been unloaded in Liverpool. An animal trainer named W. Manders bought and exhibited them in a Northhampton zoo. Below the rattlesnake cage there was a container full of hot water so that the temperature around the snakes would stay warm. Once the water started to boil too violently, and a guard approached to rearrange the burning sticks. Unfortunately, he left the cage half-open. When he returned, he noticed that one of the eight snakes had escaped. Indeed, the terrifying rattler kept leaping upwards in the middle of the zoo, hissing and threatening by thrusting up its head. People tried to capture the loose snake, which slithered into the cages of the other animals and ended up biting an enormous buffalo on the nostril. A magnificent horse from a breeding farm was harnessed to a carriage. The snake darted and bit it as well. The horse immediately started to kick out, to rear up so violently that it managed to make the reptile fall off. The horse crushed it under its shoed hooves; but a few moments after being bitten, it started shaking. Its eyes sprung out of their sockets and it started neighing plaintively. A few minutes later, it died in excruciating pain.

You, snaky charmer—what did you want to bite with your forked tongue?

Dans le bois brun, ligne tortueuse de la veine.
Destin tranché.
Bois brun de notre mort.

Matin nu
Matin cru
douloureux matin de séparation
de brisure de l'agencement du rêve.
Les rues, alors, sont toujours froides, grises, humides.

La vieille chaise, son plateau lustré par une coulure de soleil endormi venue du dehors une grande écharpe rouge suspendue à son dossier.
L'insolite se propose — et le décoratif.
Avec pareil sujet, le peintre aurait loisir d'exprimer dans un vraisemblable, c'est-à-dire un recevable pour la durée, la somme de ses troubles angoissiels — ainsi que l'ont fait des catalyseurs d'art sachant que Art et Magie sont conjoints, qu'on les détruit à prétendre les séparer.
Dynamisme de continuité que saisit le génie.

La force des attraits n'est qu'à moi seul.
Les images extérieures leur sont conformes.

Polyphème dit :
— Je suis le visionnaire des inaccomplis.

Fragile, délicate, elle dansait en robe blanche dans le clapotis des écumes. Le soleil poudreux du matin froissait d'or l'air autour d'elle, vagabonde des hasards. Elle souriait timidement en se déployant dans une suite de gestes longs et lents, mais ses yeux restaient graves, comme apeurés par cette proximité de sa faiblesse, de cette force sourde qui venait se dissoudre à ses pieds ; insaisissable signe d'une inexplicable fusion ancestrale.

Brown wood veined with tortuous lines.
A clear-cut destiny.
Brown wood of our death.

Naked morning
Raw morning
painful morning of separation
as the dream scheme is shattered.
In this case, the streets are always cold, gray, wet.

The old chair, its seat shiny in the sleepy sunlight flowing in from outside; a large red scarf is hanging over its back.

What is odd stands out—and what is decorative.

With such subject matter, the artist would have the leisure to express all his troubling anxieties as something true to life, as something acceptable over a long period of time—as did the catalysts of art who knew that Art and Magic are linked, that they are both destroyed when one attempts to separate them.

Genius grasps this dynamic continuity.

The force of attraction belongs to me alone.
Outer images conform to it.

Polyphemus says:
—I am the seer of all that remains unaccomplished.

Fragile, delicate, she was dancing in a white dress amid the lapping waves. All around this random wanderer, the powdery morning sunlight was crumpling the air with gold. She was smiling shyly while making a show of herself in a series of long slow movements, but her eyes remained solemn as if frightened because of this nearness to her own weakness, to this muted force rolling up and dissolving at her feet; the enigmatic sign of an inexplicable ancestral fusion.

Qui étais-tu, avec tes baisers, tes alanguissements, tes caresses de passage ?

Notre rencontre fut de celles qui ont forme de nuit ; imprécises, sournoises, fuyantes.

Nous ne parlâmes que fort peu, seulement à hauteur du murmure ; l'expression se faisait aussitôt étreinte.

Je n'ai souvenance que des lueurs cuivrées de la lumière sur des éclats de peau échappés au drap malmené.

Souvenir de la blessure douce du regard, de l'abandon plaintif des lèvres larges ouvertes.

Le petit jour sec se cloue d'un coup aux fenêtres.

Matin glacé.

Vase vénitien de verre jaune cannelé au col longuement élancé, ne vivant que de lumière, de transparence.

Nous flânions entre les boutiques de Venise, escortés par les enfants espérant de nous quelque charité, mieux encore, quelque tendresse ; ta beauté avait le poids de la générosité, la grandeur de la calme insolence.

Le marchand était un petit homme chauve, avec toutes les apparences de la servilité.

Ta main sur ce vase lumineux, prise assurée.

Venise — doucement endolorie.

Ton rire de jeunesse — sans pesanteur.

L'écrivain italien Francesco Lombardi mourut à cent douze ans après avoir été dans sa vie chargé par ses compatriotes de prêter en leur nom serment à Philippe V.

Nous avons déjeuné à Bari, sa ville natale, où il mourut également. Tu étais exaspérément désirable dans une robe d'une exemplaire sagesse. Un vieil homme vint auprès de nous lorsque nous nous apprêtions à nous en aller et, à brûle-pourpoint, nous entretint abondamment du Christ, les yeux embués de larmes.

Je ne pensais qu'à ton corps.

Who were you with your kisses, your languor, your passing caresses?

Our encounter was one of those that are shaped like night; vague, sly, elusive.

We spoke very little, only in murmurs; uttering anything immediately became embrace.

I recall only coppery glimmers flashing on skin uncovered by a sheet kicked away.

Memories of the soft wounded look, the plaintive way large open lips gave themselves over.

The dry dawn suddenly sticks to the windows.

Icy morning.

Venetian vase made of fluted yellow glass, with a long slender neck, nourished only by light, transparency.

We were strolling among the shops of Venice, accompanied by children hoping for alms and, even better, some tenderness; your beauty was weighty with generosity, the grandeur of calm insolence.

The shopkeeper was a small, bald, servile-looking man.

Your hand on this luminous vase, a sure catch.

Venice—with its sweet pains.

Your youthful laugh—without gravity.

The Italian writer Francesco Lombardi died at the age of one hundred twelve after having been made responsible by his compatriots, during his lifetime, for taking oaths of allegiance, in their name, to Philip V.

We had lunch in Bari, his hometown, where he also died. You were exasperatingly desirable in a dress that was a model of chastity. An old man approached as we were getting ready to leave and suddenly started talking at length about Christ, his eyes full of tears.

I was thinking only of your body.

Italie des neiges
des arbres dénudés
des longs chemins de terre enfrilosés
de canaux à l'eau noire
de l'homme qui passe dans le froid et le vide
du cri de l'oiseau noir
Italie des mages.

Veillant sur son troupeau, Polyphème voit de loin s'approcher des étrangers qu'on jurerait surgis de la mer. Sa sensibilité instantanément s'échauffe ; son cœur s'affole sans qu'il puisse à ce brusque dérangement fournir d'explication.

— Nos ennemis ont-ils une odeur ? se demande-t-il.

Il observe la troupe progressant dans sa direction. Une force incertaine l'incite à se rassurer.

— Ce n'est pas pour moi qu'ils viennent. Ce sont des étrangers, rien de plus. Une fois poussés chez moi, j'en serai maître, comme je le fus des précédents.

Toutefois, un indéfinissable malaise persiste en lui, qui lui est menace.

Ingénuité de ta nudité.

Je te grave sur l'absolu des désirs rouges.

Silhouette sombre dans le vide de l'espace. Incarnation de l'insoutenable désolation de la solitude.

Violent, le vent froid malmène ses vêtements d'une invisible main furieuse.

Il avance, un peu voûté.

Peut-être n'a-t-il pas de destination ? Peut-être est-il l'image engendrée par l'indéterminé ?

Possible forme de la mort.

Italy of snowfalls
of leafless trees
of long deeply shivering dirt paths
of canals full of black water
of the man who walks by in the cold and emptiness
of the cry of the black bird
Italy of magi.

Watching over his herd, Polyphemus spots strangers approaching from afar; one would swear they had emerged from the sea. His temper instantaneously flares; his heart panics without his being able to explain this sudden agitation.

—Do our enemies have special smell? he wonders.

He watches the troop heading toward him. A vague force prompts him to put his mind at rest.

—They aren't coming for me. They're strangers, nothing more. Once they've pushed up this far, I'll be their master as I was of the preceding ones.

However, an indefinable uneasiness persists inside him, like a threat.

Your ingenuous nudity.

I engrave you on the absolute of red desires.

Dark silhouette in the emptiness of space. Incarnation of unbearable desolate solitude.

Like a furious invisible hand, the cold violent wind blows the clothes every which way.

A little stooped over, he goes forward.

Is he perhaps heading nowhere? Is he perhaps an image born of what is indeterminate?

Possible form of death.

Il y eut l'instant où, sans question, elle m'eût suivi au bout d'elle-même.

En de semblables suspensions du temps, les secondes ont la pesanteur d'espaces inconnus rêvés.

Nos vies sont plus proches que jamais d'un éclatement poussiéreux.

Une force innovée supplante les destins.

La plus petite décision peut aboutir à l'exceptionnel, qu'il soit crime ou sublimation.

Critique d'Horace :

On s'imagine, parce que la comédie prend ses sujets dans la vie commune, que c'est une carrière bien moins épineuse ; mais Thalie a d'autant plus d'obstacles à vaincre qu'elle a moins d'indulgence à espérer. Voyez comme Plaute soutient faiblement le rôle d'un jeune homme amoureux, d'un père intéressé ou d'un astucieux entremetteur ? Et Dossénus ! comme il abuse de ses éternels parasites ! comme il arpente lourdement la scène avec son brodequin qui grimace ! C'est qu'il ne voit que les écus à empocher.

L'heure meurt.

Nous nous sommes arrêtés sur une route entre Londres et Brighton.

Il est deux, trois heures du matin.

Tu es couverte de ton gros manteau gris à ceinture.

Nous faisons quelques pas en silence.

Le ciel est étincelant.

Les constellations s'appellent Andromède, Cassiopée, Dauphin, Dragon, Hercule, Cygne, Lion, Persée, Cocher.

Tu es du signe des Gémeaux.

Ta planète est Mercure.

Tu es mercurienne.

Conrad Moricand, l'astrologue, ami du génial Henry Miller, dit que le natif des Gémeaux a des analogies avec —

le blaireau

la fouine

le merle

le geai

There was that moment when, without question, she would have followed me to the very limits of herself.

When time is suspended in such ways, seconds have the gravity of unknown dream realms.

Our lives are closer than ever to a dusty explosion.

A newly fashioned force supplants destinies.

The slightest decision can lead to something exceptional, be it crime or sublimation.

Horace's criticism:

Comedy is believed to require the least pains, because it fetches its subjects from common life; but the less indulgence it meets with, the more labor it requires. See how Plautus supports the character of a lover under age, how that of a covetous father, how those of a cheating pimp: how Dossennus exceeds all measure in his voracious parasites; with how loose a sock he runs over the stage: for he is glad to put the money in his pocket.

The hour dies.

We've stopped on a road between London and Brighton.

It's two or three o'clock in the morning.

You're wrapped in your thick gray belted coat.

We walk for a while in silence.

The sky is twinkling.

The constellations are called Andromeda, Cassiopeia, Delphinus, Draco, Hercules, Cygnus, Leo, Perseus, Charioteer.

You're a Gemini.

Your planet is Mercury.

You're mercurial.

Conrad Moricand the astrologist, who was a friend of the brilliant Henry Miller, says that a person born under the sign of Gemini has analogies with—

badgers
martens
blackbirds
jays

l'araignée
la guêpe.
Les principales étoiles sont —
Aldébaran, Algol, Castor, Mizar, Altaïr, Capella, Rigel, Régulus, Sirius, Véga.
Ma principale étoile frissonne un peu dans un gros manteau gris à ceinture.
Nous serons à Brighton au petit jour.
Il pleuvra.
Il fera frais.
La mer sera mauve.
Mrs. Slowight nous aura préparé un lit bien chaud.

L'une proche de l'autre sur la bordure de ciment de la cheminée, deux fauvettes en conversation avant le crépuscule.

Abandonnez-moi ma douleur — qui m'appartient.

— Sais-tu qui je suis ?
L'immense place princière sous la pluie.
— Je suis le fantôme de toutes tes vies.
Quelques passants courbés, rapides, à l'abri des parapluies.
— Tu m'as reconnue. Je sais que tu m'as reconnue.
Un chien réfléchissant, immobile, comme pétrifié ; peut-être perdu.
— Je viens d'aussi loin, de plus loin que toi.
L'enfilade des chambres du palais est silencieuse comme un tombeau.
— Je t'appartiens parce que je suis ton corps.
Une seconde d'inattention, le chien a disparu de la place.
— Je suis à la fois ton innocence et ton savoir.
Les tentures sont soyeuses sous la main.
Venise, ce matin, est brouillée.

Abeille citronnée au cœur de la marguerite.

spiders

wasps.

The main stars are—

Aldebaran, Algol, Castor, Mizar, Altair, Capella, Rigel, Regulus, Sirius, Vega.

My main star is shivering a little in a thick gray belted coat.

We'll be in Brighton at dawn.

It'll be raining.

It'll be cold.

The sea will be mauve.

Mrs. Slowight will have prepared a warm cozy bed for us.

Perched near each other on the cement edge of the chimney, two warblers conversing before nightfall.

Leave me my pain—it belongs to me.

—Do you know who I am?

A vast princely square in the rain.

—I am the ghostly woman of all your lives.

A few bent-over passersby walking fast, sheltered by umbrellas.

—You've recognized me. I know you've recognized me.

A dog pondering something, motionlessly, as if petrified; perhaps lost.

—I have come from as far as, from farther away than, you have.

The row of palace rooms is as silent as a grave.

—I belong to you because I am your body.

A second of inattentiveness; the dog has vanished from the square.

—I am at once your innocence and your knowledge.

The drapes are silky in my hand.

Venice is blurry this morning.

Lemony bee in the heart of the daisy.

Saignée, saignement, saigneur, saignant.
Seigneur — Seigneur — Seigneur !

Tout à l'heure, quelqu'un est allé tirer par les oreilles dans sa cage un gros lapin blanc et roux, l'a assommé d'un coup de poing sur la nuque, l'a saigné en lui arrachant un œil, son sang recueilli dans un récipient blanc, puis l'a suspendu à des crochets par les pattes postérieures pour le dépouiller de sa peau doucement veloutée et, enfin, l'a éventré, ses entrailles chaudes jetées aux chiens impatients.
Le ciel était très bleu, le mur d'en face vernissé de soleil pailleté.

Lorsqu'il veut m'éprouver, Satan me fait entendre ma mémoire.

Les trains ne partent plus, les quais de gares sont déserts, les bruits se sont fondus dans une néantisation dont nous sommes cause — nous fûmes les ultimes électrificateurs de vie.
Ce matin où, diabolique Beauté flamboyante, je contemplais ton spectacle magnétique.
Tu marchais dans un pantalon ajusté avec l'assurance du passage obligé ; brutale de jeunesse, de futures éclosions ; si forte l'intensité en toi que nul homme n'osait te regarder ; devenue brillance.
Nous avions sans dormir passé la nuit dans un grand hôtel. Liberté provisoire, j'étais l'accompagnateur de ton intrépidité. Tout autour de nous devenait défi paradoxal. Flottait dans notre approche des éléments épars d'une supra-normalité.
Tu m'avais, ce jour-là, demandé si je connaissais la science de l'œil — oui, celle de t'admirer.

— Je renaîtrai de tout ce qui n'est pas évasion, se convainc Polyphème dans sa cécité nouvelle.

Bloodletting, bleeding, bloodletter, bloody, blordy.
Lord—Lord—Lord!

A short while ago, someone went to pull out, from its cage, a big white and russet rabbit by his ears, killed it by bringing down his fist on the nape of its neck, bled it by ripping out an eye, collecting the blood in a white container, then hung it up by its hind legs from hooks in order to strip it of its soft velvety skin and, finally, disemboweled it, tossing the warm entrails to impatient dogs.

The sky was bright blue, the wall across the way glazed with speckles of sunlight.

When he wants to test me, Satan has me listen to my memory.

The trains no longer leave, the station platforms are deserted, noises have blended into an annihilation we have caused—we were the last electrifiers of life.

That morning when I watched your mesmerizing show, you diabolical flamboyant Beauty.

You were wearing a pair of well-fitting pants because you knew where you'd have to walk; you were brutally youthful, ready to blossom; so strongly intense that no man dared to glance; you had become brilliance.

We had spent a sleepless night in a big hotel. Temporarily free, I escorted your boldness. Everything around us became a paradoxical challenge. Scattered supra-normal elements were hovering in our approach.

That day, you had asked me if I knew the science of the eye—yes, that of admiring you.

—I will be born again of all that is not escape, Polyphemus convinces himself, now that he is blind.

Il a plu la nuit durant. En bas, vue depuis la fenêtre, la rue est jaunâtre d'humidité. Il y a des sillonnements de passants flous.

On imagine la frilosité, une engourdissante réfraction nerveuse.

Elle pourrait accourir dans cette brunosité délayée.

Apparaître à l'extrémité du trottoir marbré.

Lointaine encore, mais identifiable, comme elle sait l'être.

À la fois fluette et d'une force certaine.

Serrée à la taille dans un long imperméable de couleur passée.

La moindre des fibrilles d'elle-même sachant que la minute n'est à rien d'autre, ne saurait à rien d'autre être consacrée qu'à me rejoindre dans cette défense de murs qui, déjà, ont été nos protecteurs.

Londres a sommeil.

Tes éclosions d'insouciante jeunesse dans les rues endolories.

L'hôtel dépourvu de clients surplombe la plage vide. Grand vent. Sable coupant dans l'air. Enragement de la mer. Voix grognante. Brusques placages liquides. Je suis un promeneur. Un solitaire. Un évadé. Je n'attends plus de moi d'étonnement. Importe la capacité de marcher, de le savoir, de le vouloir — celle-ci ou une autre, les destinations n'ont pas de sens. Arpenter la plage, escalader les rochers, devenir celui qui est allé plus loin — autant d'inutilités. Seul le pouvoir faire a ses vertus. Je me commande, m'ordonne, me domine, sachant que rien n'a de valeur que ce qui est commandé, ordonné, dominé. Mes traces sont imprimées dans le sable. Quelques minutes, elles n'y seront plus. Bientôt, je chercherai dans la petite ville grelottante un endroit où m'abriter, où me mettre au chaud. Je boirai du café. Si l'endroit me convient, peut-être y déjeunerai-je. Je ne repartirai qu'ensuite, avant la nuit. J'ai voulu échapper. Escapade dénuée d'ambition. Élan avorté de moi-même, comme tant d'autres. L'hôtel aux vieux volets verts clos est lui aussi profondément mortel.

Luna. Lune. Diane. Artémis. Astarté. Europe.

Ne crains rien. Endors-toi.

It rained all night long. Seen from the window, the street below is wet and yellowish. Blurry pedestrians are walking straight ahead.

The shivering and a numbing nervous refraction can be imagined.

She could rush up to me in this thinned-out brownish light.

Appear at the end of the marbled sidewalk.

Still afar but recognizable, as she knows how to be.

Both slender and full of force.

A long faded raincoat tightly belted around her waist.

Her slightest fibrils knowing that the present moment is, and can only be, devoted exclusively to meeting me within these rampart-like walls that have already protected us.

London is sleepy.

Your carefree youth blossoming time and again in the aching streets.

The guestless hotel overlooks the empty beach. Strong wind. Sharp grains of sand in the air. Raging sea. Groaning voice. Liquid suddenly smashing up. I am walking. All alone. An escapee. I no longer expect to be astonished. What matters is the ability to walk, to know I am walking, to want to walk—all destinations are meaningless. Pacing up and down the beach, scaling rocky cliffs, becoming the person who has gone further; these goals are all pointless. Only being able to do things has its virtues. I command myself, order myself, dominate myself, knowing that only what is commanded, ordered, and dominated is worth anything. My tracks are engraved in the sand. In a few minutes, they will no longer be there. I will soon seek warmth and shelter in the shivering little town. I will drink coffee. If the place suits me, perhaps I will have lunch there. I will leave only later, before nightfall. I wanted to escape. Escape devoid of ambition. Aborted élan of myself, like so many others. The hotel with its old green closed shutters is also extremely deadly.

Luna. Moon. Diana. Artemis. Astarte. Europa.
Fear nothing. Fall asleep.

NOTES

(p. 25) First epigraph: The English version is drawn from *The Stromata* (Book 5) by Saint Clement of Alexandria, translated by Rev. William Wilson, M.A., text edited by Rev. Alexander Roberts and James Donaldson and first published by T&T Clark in Edinburgh in 1867.

(p. 25) Second epigraph: Calaferte found this quotation in Carl Gustav Jung's *Psychologie et alchemie*, Paris: Buchet-Chastel, 1970, p. 309, note 13 (about the hermetic *Tractatus aureus*, 6, I, p. 442, attributed to Hermes Trimegistus). For an English explanation of the same quotation, see Jung's *Dreams*, translated from the German by R. F. C. Hull, Princeton, New Jersey: Princeton University Press, 1974, p. 202, note 44. The translation of the Latin phrase is "One thing in one circle or vessel." Some of Jung's explanation perhaps elucidates the structure of and the vision behind *The Violet Blood of the Amethyst*: "The circumambulation has its parallel in the [. . .] 'circulation of spirits or circular distillation, that is, the outside to the inside, the inside to the outside, likewise the lower and the upper; and when they meet together in one circle, you could no longer recognize what was outside or inside, or lower or upper; but all would be *one thing in one circle or vessel* [my italics]. For this vessel is the true philosophical Pelican, and there is no other to be sought for in all the world.'" Jung also cites the *Rosarium*: "Out of man and woman make a round circle and extract the quadrangle from this and from the quadrangle the triangle. Make a round circle and you will have the philosopher's stone" (*ibid.*).

(p. 29) *Serpentaire*, etc. Strictly speaking, the passage is untranslatable, so I have retained the French words, provided equivalents in most cases, and rendered the definitions. Calaferte was interested in these specific words. Alternative translations would list compound English nouns based on the roots "snake" or "serpent."

(p. 31) ". . . in this vacant Italy where only death and eroticism become husband and wife." This is the first of several reverences to Italy. It is perhaps noteworthy that Calaferte was born in Turin and was of Italian origin. But he was raised in Lyon and always wrote in French.

(p. 33) "With innocent simplicity, Phaedrus . . ." Calaferte is citing the *Fables* of the Latin writer Caius Julius Phaedrus (15 B.C.–50 A.D.). By imitating Aesop, Phaedrus introduced the genre into Roman literature. The quotation comes from Book II, Fable VII: "The Mules and the Robbers": "Laden with burdens, two Mules were travelling along; the one was carrying baskets with money, the other sacks distended with store of barley. The former, rich with his burden, goes exulting along, with neck erect, and tossing to-and-fro upon his throat *his* clear-toned bell: his companion follows, with quiet and easy step. Suddenly some Robbers rush from ambush upon them, and amid the slaughter pierce the Mule with a sword, and carry off the money; the valueless barley they neglect. While, then, the one despoiled was bewailing their mishaps: 'For my part,' says the other, 'I am glad I was thought so little of; for I have lost nothing, nor have I received hurt by a wound.' According to the moral of this Fable, poverty is safe; great riches are liable to danger." (*The Fables of Phaedrus*, translated by Henry Thomas Riley and Christopher Smart, London: George Bell and Sons, 1887.)

(p. 35) "The soul between God and the Devil." In French, an expression for twilight is "entre chien et loup" (between dog and wolf).

(p. 41) "My Lady, do not be displeased . . ." From Jean-Baptiste La Curne de Sainte-Palaye's *Mémoire de l'ancienne Chevalerie considérée comme un établissement politique et militaire*, Paris, 1759–1780, 3 volumes. La Curne de Sainte-Palaye (1697–1781) was a French historian and philologist.

(p. 47) "Down fall the ash trees, the knotty holm-oak is hurled down . . ." From *The Pharsalia of Lucan*, translation H. T. Riley, London: H. G. Bohn, 1853, book 3 (440ff.). Calaferte cites a French translation evoking "ormes" (elms), but Riley correctly interprets the Latin "orni" as "ashes," which I have modified to "ash trees" for clarity here. Lucan (Marcus Annaeus Lucanus) was a Roman writer (39–65). After participating in the Gaius Calpurnius Piso conspiracy against Nero (37–68), the Roman emperor infamous for his extravagance and acts of treachery, he was forced to commit suicide. Tacitus (*Annals* XV, 70, 1) reports the anecdote about Lucan's reciting of lines from his poetry as his last words. In the next passage, Calaferte makes the slight error of stating that Lucan (39–65) dies at the age of twenty-seven; I have interpreted this as "in [his] twenty-seventh year." Dodona is a site located in Epirus, in northwestern Greece. There was an oracle there associated with a Mother Goddess. Considered to be the oldest such shrine in Hellenic Greece, Dodona had an oak tree whose rustling would be interpreted by priests and priestesses. Michel de Montaigne (1533–1592) is, of course, the famous French essayist.

(p. 49) "A mystery to myself." The indeed mysterious French original, "À moi-même mystère," perhaps also echoes Saint Augustine's "quaestio mihi factus sum" (I have become a question for myself), *Confessions* X, 33.

(p. 53) "hand of a woman of Kos / who mixed gold into the weighty fabrics embellishing the body of young Nemesis". The Greek island Kos is located in the Dodecanese. In Greek mythology, Nemesis personifies indignation and divine vengeance against hubris and arrogance (towards the gods). She is variously described as the daughter of Oceanus of Zeus, of Erebus and Nyx, or of Nyx (Night) alone.

(p. 55) "Our alliances are mathematical." Note that the French word "alliance" also means "wedding ring."

(p. 55) "The merry science." The French title of Friedrich Nietzsche's *Fröhliche Wissenschaft* (1882) is *Le gai savoir*, so Calaferte is intentionally making a distinction. He is in fact thinking of a medieval term for poetry and poetic gatherings in which knights and lady poets debated questions dealing with gallantry. The term used also refers to the poetry of the troubadours.

(p. 57) Michele Mercati was an Italian humanist. He was a friend of Marsile Ficin (1433–1499), who was a poet and philosopher. In the Gallimard edition, Calaferte errs by evoking Sixtus V; the pope at the time was Alexander VI (1431–1503), who served between 1492 and 1503. Calaferte's source is Baronius, in the *Giornale de' letterati*, volume XXIX. The Latin phrase means approximately: "Those things are really true!"

(p. 59) "I heard a Fly buzz . . ." This poem by Emily Dickinson (1830–1886) was probably written in 1862 and was published posthumously in 1896. Calaferte was an admirer of Dickinson. His translation manuscript, *55 Poèmes d'Emily Dickinson*, remains unpublished. This specific poem was not included in the manuscript. Published as poem 465 in *The Complete Poems of Emily Dickinson* (edited by Thomas H. Johnson, Boston / New York / London / Toronto: Little, Brown and Company, 1960), the entire poem reveals themes also present in *The Violet Blood of the Amethyst*:

> I heard a Fly buzz—when I died—
> The Stillness in the Room
> Was like the Stillness in the Air—
> Between the Heaves of Storm—
>
> The Eyes around—had wrung them dry—
> And Breaths were gathering firm
> For that last Onset—when the King
> Be witnessed—in the Room—
>
> I willed my Keepsakes—Signed away
> What portion of me be
> Assignable—and then it was
> There interposed a Fly—
> With Blue—uncertain stumbling Buzz—
>
> Between the light—and me—
> And then the Windows failed—and then
> I could not see to see—

(p. 59) The poem by William Blake (1757–1827) is entitled "Earth's Answer" and is included in Songs of Experience (1794):

> Earth rais'd up her head
> From the darkness dread and drear.
> Her light fled:
> Stony dread!
> And her locks cover'd with grey despair.
>
> "Prison'd on wat'ry shore,
> Starry Jealousy dos keep my den
> Cold and hoar;
> Weeping o'er,
> I hear the father of the ancient men.
>
> "Selfish father of men,
> Cruel, jealous, selfish fear:
> Can delight,
> Chain'd in night,
> The virgins of youth and morning bear?

"Does spring hide its joy
When buds and blossoms grow?
Does the sower
Sow by night?
Or the plowman in darkness plow?

"Break this heavy chain
That does freeze my bones around.
Selfish! vain!
Eternal bane!
That free Love with bondage bound."

(p. 61) King Nebuchadnezzar (634–562 B.C.) was the king of the Neo-Babylonian Empire. See especially the Book of Daniel (2:31ff.).

(p. 67) "Terra habitatur et quiescit." The Latin phrase is found in Zechariah 1:11: "And they answered the angel, of the Lord that stood among the myrtle trees, and said, We have walked to and fro through the earth, and, behold, all the earth sitteth still, and is at rest."

(p. 69) "Smart in a long-napped toga . . ." The translation of this poem (Book II, LVIII) is by Walter C. A. Ker, *Martial: Epigrams*, Loeb Classical Library, London: Heinemann / New York: Putnam's Sons, 1919. Martial (40–104) was a Roman poet known for his satirical epigrams. Zoilus of Amphipolis (400 B.C.–320 B.C.) was a Greek poet and philosopher known for this harsh criticism of Homer. He took on the name "Homeromastix" (Homer-Whipper).

(p. 73) "Venice—*city of bells and churches*." A quotation of a half-line nearly at the end of the poetic sequence "Italia mia" (*Le Roman inachevé*) by the French poet Louis Aragon (1897–1982): "Ville de verre et de chaleur ville de cloches et d'églises / Ville de cris et de voleurs de putains et d'écornifleurs" (*Oeuvres poétiques completes*, volume II, Paris: Gallimard, 2007, p. 202).

(p. 73) "First and foremost, a lady or maiden lady . . ." The passage, from *Le Parement et le triomphe des dames d'honneur* (1510), is by Olivier de la Marche (1426–1502), a French poet, chronicler, and soldier.

(p. 75) *Ecce Adam, quasi unus ex nobis factus est, sciens bonum et malum*. From the Latin Vulgate Bible, Genesis 3:22: "Behold, the man is become as one of us, to know good and evil."

(p. 77) Mencius, the Chinese philosopher and teacher of Confucianism, probably lived between 372 and 289 B.C. An ox is going to be sacrificed so that its blood can consecrate a bell. As the ox passes by, the king notices that it is frightened, says that it is like an innocent person being led to slaughter, and asks that it be released. The man leading the ox to the sacrifice then asks whether the bell should not be consecrated. The king says that a sheep can be used instead. Mencius then retorts: "If you felt pained by its being led without guilt to the place of death, what was there to choose between an ox and a sheep?"

(p. 79) "It is made lawful for you to go unto your wives . . ." *Koran*, Sûrah II, 187. See *The Meaning of the Glorious Koran*, translated by Mohammed Marmaduke Pickthall, New York / Toronto: New American Library and London: The New English Library, 1931.

(p. 79) Seshat. The Egyptian goddess of writing, astronomy, astrology, architecture, mathematics. She was later considered to be the daughter, wife, or consort of Thoth, the god of wisdom.

(p. 81) "Open thy mouth wide, and I will fill it." Psalm 81:10.

(p. 83) "Someone wearily walks up the stairway of the apartment building, repeating the German word *Kloster*." "Kloster" means "monastery" or "convent."

(p. 83) "I started Early —Took my dog— . . ." This poem (written in 1862 and published in 1891) is No. 520 in the aforementioned edition of Emily Dickinson's poetry. Calaferte's translation (in the Gallimard edition of *Le Sang violet de l'améthyste*) was later modified into this definitive version: "Je partis de bon matin — J'emmenai mon chien — / Et j'allai voir la mer — / Étonnées les Sirènes quittèrent les profondeurs / Pour savoir qui j'étais —." In English, the entire poem reads:

> I started Early—Took my Dog—
> And visited the Sea—
> The Mermaids in the Basement
> Came out to look at me—
>
> And Frigates—in the Upper Floor—
> Extended Hempen Hands—
> Presuming Me to be a Mouse—
> Aground—upon the Sands—
>
> But no Man moved me—till the Tide
> Went past my simple Shoe—
> And past my Apron—and my Belt
> And past my Bodice—too—
>
> And made as He would eat me up—
> As wholly as a Dew
> Upon a Dandelion's Sleeve—
> And then—I started—too—
>
> And He—He followed—close behind—
> I felt His Silver Heel
> Upon my Ankle—Then my Shoes
> Would overflow with Pearl—
>
> Until We met the Solid Town—
> No One He seemed to know—
> And bowing—with a Mighty look—
> At me—The Sea withdrew—

(p. 85) Propertius, the Roman poet, was born between 54 B.C. and 43 B.C. (and probably in 47 B.C.) and died in 16 B.C. or 15 B.C. The line is found at the beginning of Elegy XXXIII, Book II: "Quae dea tam cupidos totiens diuisit amantis, / quaecumque illa fuit, semper amara fuit." A more literal translation would be: "Whoever she was, that goddess who split up lovers so often was always bitter."

(p. 91) Lilith is considered to be Adam's first wife, before Eve, and essentially to be the First Woman. She is often depicted as a nocturnal and demonic being. See "screech owl," which renders "lilith," in Isaiah 34:14: "The wild beasts of the desert shall also meet with the wild beasts of the island, and the satyr shall cry to his fellow; the screech owl also shall rest there, and find for herself a place of rest."

(p. 93) Vasily Vasilyevich Rozanov (1856–1919), a controversial Russian philosopher. Calaferte draws his quotation from *Esseulement*, translated by Jacques Michaut, Lausanne: L'Age d'Homme, 1980.

(p. 93) Hermogenes of Tarsos was a Greek rhetorician, nicknamed The Polisher, who was active during the Roman Emperor Marcus Aurelius's reign (161–180 A.D.). His brain damage probably resulted from meningitis.

(p. 95) William Collins (1721–1759) was an English poet. The lines are from the second stanza of his "Ode on the Poetical Character" (1747).

(p. 95) "How did I hear your gaze?" The French verb *entendre* can mean "to hear, to listen" and "to understand." Because of synaesthetic imagery elsewhere in the book, the former solution seems justifiable here.

(p. 97) "Shylock consents to lend money." The anecdote is taken from Shakespeare's play *The Merchant of Venice*.

(p. 97) "It will be Summer—eventually. / Ladies—with parasols — . . ." Written in 1862 and published only in 1929, this poem by Emily Dickinson is No. 342 in the aforementioned edition. Calaferte left an unpublished version of it. The entire poem:

> It will be Summer—eventually.
> Ladies—with parasols—
> Sauntering Gentlemen—with Canes—
> And little Girls—with Dolls—
>
> Will tint the pallid landscape—
> As 'twere a bright Bouquet—
> Tho' drifted deep, in Parian—
> The Village lies—today—
>
> The Lilacs—bending many a year—
> Will sway with purple load—
> The Bees—will not despise the tune—
> Their Forefathers—have hummed—

> The Wild Rose—redden in the Bog—
> The Aster—on the Hill
> Her everlasting fashion—set—
> And Covenant Gentians—frill—
>
> Till Summer folds her miracle—
> As Women—do—their Gown—
> Or Priests—adjust the Symbols—
> When Sacrament—is done.

(p. 99) "To free oneself from what is never but alignment . . ." In the Gallimard edition, the French reads: "Se délivrer de ce qui n'est pas alignement . . ." The manuscript has revealed that this should read: "Se délivrer de ce qui n'est jamais qu'alignement . . ."

(p. 99) "To free oneself from all that is not clairvoyance, magic, miracle." In the Gallimard edition, the French reads: "Se délivrer de ce qui n'est pas croyance, magie, miracle." Close inspection of the manuscript has revealed that "croyance" should be "voyance." Note that a phrase from this sentence, quoted from the Gallimard edition, is used as the title of my second essay on Calaferte, "'Belief, Magic, Miracle': Louis Calaferte as Poet," *Paths to Contemporary French Literature*, volume 2, New Brunswick, New Jersey / London: Transaction Publishers, 2007, pp. 185–198.

(p. 99) "Always deluded in its hopes, the human heart . . ." Leopardi (1798–1837), the Italian poet and philosopher. *Zibaldone*, 2316.

(p. 101) "*Corpo celestiale*." The concept of a "heavenly body" or "celestial body" shows up in several esoteric traditions.

(p. 103) "Sea—eternity." It is impossible for a French reader to read the two French words together without thinking of Arthur Rimbaud's lines from *A Season in Hell*: "Elle est retrouvée! / Quoi? L'éternité / C'est la mer mêlée / Au soleil." Mark Treharne translates: "Rediscovered once more? / Ah yes! Eternity: / The mingled light / Of sun and sea" (*A Season in Hell and Illuminations*, London: J. M. Dent, 1998).

(p. 105) "Vivaldi's deeply moving necromantic music." The Italian composer (1678–1741).

(p. 113) Geoffroy de Rudel, or Jaufré Rudel, was a troubadour born around 1113. One of his most famous poems was indeed "l'amor de luenh," written in Occitan and dedicated to a Middle-Eastern princess. He died around 1162, on a crusade.

(p. 113) Gaia. As the Mother Goddess, Gaia personifies the earth in Hesiodic cosmogony. She is the maternal ancestor of monsters and the divine races.

(p. 117) "Sono solo [. . .] E più niente." "I am alone / I am alone / I am alone / And nothing more."

(p. 119) Macías (ca. 1340–1370) was a Galician troubadour. Several legends about his amatory prowess remain attached to his name. In a version different from the one evoked by Calaferte, the jealous husband sticks a lance through a hole in the ceiling of the cell and kills the poet.

(p. 119) Luís de Camões (ca. 1524–1580) is the most famous Portuguese poet. Of his works, *The Lusiads* is the best known. In the Gallimard edition, Calaferte uses the obsolete French spelling, "Camoens."

(p. 121) "It was midnight, and The Cid . . ." Rodrigo Díaz de Vivar (1043–1099), known as El Cid Campeador ("The lord-master of military arts"), is a famous Spanish hero. The name of his steed was Babieca. According to legend, The Cid was offered all the best foals in the region; he chose one, however, that seemed mediocre. The priest called him "babieca" (stupid), and the horse was given this name. Tisona / Tizona is The Cid's sword. Calaferte's source is *Le Romancero espagnol ou Recueil des chants populaires de l'Espagne*, translated by M. Damas Hinard, Paris, 1884.

(p. 121) "*I will walk at night near my dead lover.*" The remark also refers to The Cid. He tells his lover, Chimène, to accompany the funereal procession, if he dies, to San Pedro de Cardena. In the Gallimard edition, the French reads: "Je marcherai la nuit près de mon amant noir." The manuscript reveals that this should be: ". . . mon amant mort."

(p. 123) Mammon refers to material greed and is often personified as a deity in Biblical literature. Note Matthew 6:19–21, 24, for example: "Lay not up for yourselves treasures upon earth, where moth and rust doth corrupt, and where thieves break through and steal: But lay up for yourselves treasures in heaven, where neither moth nor rust doth corrupt, and where thieves do not break through nor steal: For where your treasure is, there will your heart be also. [. . .] No one can serve two masters, for either he will hate the one and love the other; or else he will be devoted to one and despise the other. You can not serve both God and mammon."

(p. 123) Girolama Savonarola (1452–1498) was a Dominican priest and the instigator of the theocratic dictatorship of Florence (1494–1498). He was infamous for burning books and works of art, and for preaching against moral corruption.

(p. 123) "C'è une città di questo mondo / ma cosi bella, ma cosi strana . . ." "It is a city of this world / but how beautiful, but how strange." These lines were written by Diego Valeri (1887–1976), an Italian poet who often wrote about Venice.

(p. 129) In the Rig Veda, Indra is the Hindu God of war, storms, and rainfall.

(p. 131) "Propertius's cry." (For the Roman poet, see above.) The quoted line is the opening of Elegy VIII, Book I. Cynthia, who was Propertius's lover, is evoked in many of his poems.

(p. 133) "What is man?" The lines are quoted from the *Dialogue* of Alcuin of York (730s or 740s—804) and Pepin, the eldest son of Charlemagne.

(p. 135) "—What is this gift of creation that has reduced me to a few straight lines?" The manuscript reveals a missing "est" in the Gallimard edition: "— Quel [est] ce don de création qui m'a réduit à quelques droites?"

(p. 137) "Cum tu, Lydia, Telephi [ceruicem roseam] . . ." From Horace's *Odes*, Book 1, 13. See *The Works of Horace*, translated by Christopher Smart, revised by Theodore Alois

Buckley, New York / Cincinnati / Chicago: American Book Company, 1902. The entire passage: "O Lydia, when you commend Telephus' rosy neck, and the waxen arms of Telephus, alas! my inflamed liver swells with bile difficult to be repressed. Then neither is my mind firm, nor does my color maintain a certain situation: and the involuntary tears glide down my cheek, proving with what lingering flames I am inwardly consumed. I am on fire, whether quarrels rendered immoderate by wine have stained your fair shoulders; or whether the youth, in his fury, has impressed with his teeth a memorial on your lips."

(p. 139) "I have never felt myself live except when I am in love . . ." From Leopardi's *Zibaldone*, 59.

(p. 149) The expression "Not everyone is able to go to Corinth" is said to derive from the former wealth of the ancient Greek town and means that not everyone is able to live there; more generally, that not everyone is equal. The equivalent Latin saying is "non licet omnibus adire Corinthum" or, as Horace phrases it differently in his *Epistles* (Book 1, 17, 36): "Non cuiuis homini contingit adire Corinthum." In the aforementioned edition of *The Works of Horace*, Christopher Smart translates this as: "It is not every man's lot to gain Corinth." Calaferte is alluding to the story—told by Allus Gellius in his *Attic Nights* (Book I, VIII)—of the orator Demosthenes and the courtesan Lais (who was from Corinth). This passage of the *Attic Nights* recounts the anecdote: Sotion, a man of the Peripatetic school, was far from unknown. He wrote a book filled with wide and varied information and called it *The Horn of Amaltheia*, which is about equivalent to *The Horn of Plenty*. In that book is found the following anecdote: "Lais of Corinth," Sotion says, "used to gain a great deal of money by the grace and charm of her beauty, and was frequently visited by wealthy men from all over Greece; but no one was received who did not give what she demanded, and her demands were extravagant enough." Sotion says that this was the origin of the proverb common among the Greeks, "Not everyone is able to go to Corinth," for in vain would any man go to Corinth to visit Lais who could not pay her price. Sotion adds: "The great Demosthenes approached her secretly and asked for her favors. But Lais demanded ten thousand drachmas"—a sum equivalent in our money to ten thousand denarii. "Amazed and shocked at the woman's great impudence and the vast sum of money demanded (for a single drachma was equivalent to the daily wage of a laborer), Demosthenes turned away, remarking as he left her: 'I will not buy regret at such a price.'" "But the Greek words which he is said to have used are neater, literally meaning: 'I will not buy regret for ten thousand drachmas.'" Adapted from Allus Gellius, *Attic Nights*, translated by J. C. Rolfe, Loeb Classical Library, 1927 (revised 1946 edition).

(p. 149) "At the Scuola Ricetti." The Italian lines mean: "Spring grace / a feather of poetry / whiter, lighter / than a cassia flower."

(p. 149) "Alas, you need a heart of iron, Cornutus, to remain in the city." The opening lines of an elegy by Tibullus's (Book II, 3) "Rura meam, Cornute [Cerinthe], tenent uillaeque puellam; / ferreus est, heu! heu! Quisquis in urbe manet." Some older versions indeed use Cerinthus for Cornutus, though the latter is now acknowledged as the correct name (see Tibulle, *Élégies*, translated by Max Ponchot, Paris: Les Belles Lettres, 1926, 1989.)

(p. 151) "Io / my melancholic of the meadows." The Greek goddess Io was a priestess for Hera in Argos and a nymph. Zeus raped her and changed her into a heifer so that she would not be noticed. Hera had a guardian watch the heifer, but Hermes killed him. Plagued by the sting of a gadfly, the heifer roamed the world. The story is told by Aeschylus in *Prometheus Bound* and by Ovid in *Metamorphoses*.

(p. 151) "There's nothing sillier than a silly laugh." In Catullus's Latin: "Risu inepto res ineptior nulla est". Carmen 39, line 16.

(p. 151) "You want me to honor you, Sextus." Martial, II, LV. My translation reflects Calaferte's French. There are many other translations of this poem; for example, by James Michie, Martial, *The Epigrams*, Penguin Classics, 1972: "I wanted to love you: you prefer / To have me as your courtier. / Well, I must follow your direction. / But goodbye, Sextus, to affection."

(p. 153) "Apuleius's contradictory cross. *Alterutrae*." Apuleius (125–180) was a Latin writer and the author of *Metamorphoses* (or *The Golden Ass*). The key term "alterutrae" means "alternates" but is used by Apuleius (in his logical treatise, *Peri Hermeneias*) in the sense of "contraries," "opposites," "contradictions." See the detailed discussion of Apuleius's "Square of Opposition" in David Londey and Carmen Johanson's *The Logic of Apuleius*, Leiden: E. J. Brill, 1987.

(p. 157) "To be alive—is Power." Written in 1863, first published in 1914, this poem is No. 677 in the aforementioned edition of *The Complete Poems of Emily Dickinson*. Calaferte did not translate the poem:

> To be alive—is Power—
> Existence—in itself—
> Without a further function—
> Omnipotence—Enough—
>
> To be alive—and Will!
> 'Tis able as a God—
> The Maker—of Ourselves—be what—
> Such being Finitude!

(p. 157) "Now there was a day when the sons of God." Job 1:6–9.

(p. 157) "Daughter of Cadmus." In Greek mythology, Cadmus was a Phoenician prince. He was sent by his parents (King Agenor and Queen Telephassa of Tyre) to rescue his sister Europa after she had been abducted from Phoenicia by Zeus. Herodotus, among others, credits Cadmus with having introduced the Phoenician alphabet to the Greeks. He founded the Greek city of Thebes. With his wife Harmonia, he had four daughters (Ino, Semele, Agave, Autonoë). The four sisters are all victims of violent acts.

(p. 161) "Crimen relinquit vitae . . ." "Who desires to die leaves a stain on his life." Pubilius Syrus (85 B.C.–43 B.C.) was a Roman poet who had originally been brought to Rome as a slave. Several other translations of this maxim are possible, for example: "Eagerness for death bequeaths an indictment of life." (*Minor Latin Poets*, translated by J. Wight Duff, London: Heinemann / Harvard: Harvard University Press, 1934).

(p. 161) The Greek word *kokkos* more directly means "seed", "pit (of fruit)", "*cochenile* (mealybug, scale insect, cochineal)." The French *coccinelle* ("ladybug") comes from scientific Latin *coccinella*, from Latin *coccinus* ("scarlet"), modeled on Greek *kokkinos* "insect providing red die" (the mealybug); *kokkinos* comes from *kokkos*.

(p. 165) "Unbearably angelic face in the concert hall while the orchestra interprets Schubert's seemly distress." The Austrian composer Franz Schubert (1797–1828).

(p. 165) "Venus changes Adonis into a red anemone." Ovid, *Metamorphoses*, X, 731.

(p. 165) "*Sol invictus*." Invincible Sun. The sun god of the later Roman empire. But Calaferte is thinking of the emblem of Christ in which twelve rays depict the apostles.

(p. 167) "I could write down lines of words without consequence . . ." The Gallimard edition reads: "Je pourrais écrire des lignes de notes sans suite . . ." The manuscript reveals that "notes" should be "mots."

(p. 173) "Annua vererunt Cerealis tempora sacri ; / Secubat in vacuo sola puella toro." "Here is the yearly festival of Ceres come round again: / and my lady has to sleep in a lonely bed." In the Gallimard edition, "Cerealis" is missing from the first line and has been restored here. Ovid, *The Loves*, Book 3, Elegy X, 1–2.

(p. 173) "Orco, the Ogre." "Orco is the Italian word for "ogre." Calaferte is perhaps thinking of the Tomba dell'orco, a fourth century B.C. Etruscan burial chamber in Tarquinia, Italy. The entrance to the Tomb of Orcos II has a painting of a Cyclops, possibly Polyphemus. When this tomb was first discovered, the hairy bearded giant on the painting was mistaken for Orcus, a Roman god of the underworld who is also associated in Italian folkore with an ogre, a fairytale monster who eats human beings.

(p. 179) "*Caeci sunt oculi, quum animus alias res agit.*" "The eyes are blind when the mind is otherwise occupied." See the note above for Pubilius Syrus.

(p. 179) Thomas Chatterton (1752–1770) was an English poet, the author of pseudo-medieval works.

(p. 179) Edward Young (1681–1765) was an English poet. His *The Complaint*, or *Night Thoughts on Life, Death and Immortality* was first published in 1742, and then followed by other "Nights," in 1745. His stepdaughter died in 1736 and her husband and the poet's wife died in 1740. These three deaths are thought to have inspired *Night Thoughts*. Young was thus older than Calaferte states when the deaths occurred.

(p. 181) James Thomson (1700–1748) was a Scottish poet famous for writing the lyrics of *Rule, Britannia*. His long poems "Winter" (1726), "Summer" (1727), "Spring" (1728), and "Autumn" (1730) compose his most famous work, *The Seasons*. Actually, he had written and published some verse before arriving in London in February, 1725. He probably wrote "Winter" in May of the same year.

(p. 185) "Rise up, my love, my fair one, and come away!" Song of Solomon 2:10–13.

(p. 185) "Let me see thy countenance." Song of Solomon 2:14.

(p. 191) Francesco Lombardi (1631–1743) was an Italian writer. Philip V (1683–1746) was the King of Spain (1700–1724).

(p. 195) "Comedy is believed to require the least pains." Horace's *Epistles*, Book II, 1 ("To Augustus"). See the aforementioned edition of *The Works of Horace*. "Palute," a misprint in the Gallimard edition, has been restored to "Plaute" (Plautus) here.

(p. 195) Conrad Moricand (1887–1954) was a well-known French astrologist who wrote books on the subject and also consorted with Max Jacob, Jean Cocteau, Blaise Cendrars, and Amedeo Modigliani. He met Henry Miller in 1935 and they became close friends. Miller recalls him in *Big Sur and the Oranges of Hieronymus Bosch*. Miller was an important literary figure for Calaferte.

(p. 199) "Bloodletting, bleeding, bloodletter, bloody, blordy. / Lord—Lord—Lord!" It is impossible to reproduce the pun of "saigneur" (bloodletter) and "Seigneur" (Lord), so I'm taking some liberties here.

(p. 201) Luna, Diane, Artemis, and Astarte are goddesses who are all associated with the moon in Roman or Greek mythology; and associated with Astarte is Europa, according to Lucian of Samostata: "There is likewise in Phoenicia a temple of great size owned by the Sidonians. They call it the temple of Astarte. I hold this Astarte to be no other than the moon-goddess. But according to the story of one of the priests this temple is sacred to Europa, the sister of Cadmus. She was the daughter of Agenor, and on her disappearance from Earth the Phoenicians honored her with a temple and told a sacred legend about her; how that Zeus was enamored of her for her beauty, and changing his form into that of a bull carried her off into Crete." Lucian, *The Syrian Goddess*, translated by Herbert A. Strong and John Garstang, 1913.

BIBLIOGRAPHY

NOVELS, NARRATIVES, SHORT PROSE
Requiem des innocents, Paris: Julliard, 1952, 1994 / Paris: Gallimard-Folio, 2001.
Partage des vivants, Paris: Julliard, 1953 / Saint-Benoît-du-Sault: Tarabuste, 2011.
Septentrion, Paris: Tchou, 1963 / Paris: Denoël, 1984 / Paris: Gallimard-Folio, 1990.
No Man's Land, Paris: Julliard, 1963 / Paris: Gallimard-L'Arpenteur, 2005.
Satori, Paris: Denoël, 1968 / Paris: Gallimard-Folio, 1997.
Rosa mystica, Paris: Denoël, 1968 / Paris: Gallimard-Folio, 1996.
Portrait de l'enfant, Paris: Denoël, 1969.
Hinterland, Paris: Denoël, 1971.
Limitrophe, Paris: Denoël, 1972.
La vie parallèle, Paris: Denoël, 1974.
Épisodes de la vie des mantes religieuses, Paris: Denoël, 1976.
Campagnes, Paris: Denoël, 1979.
Ébauche d'un autoportrait, Paris: Denoël, 1983.
Promenade dans un parc, Paris: Denoël, 1987 / Paris: Gallimard-L'Imaginaire, 2011.
L'incarnation, Paris: Denoël, 1987.
Memento mori, Paris: Gallimard-L'Arpenteur, 1988.
La mécanique des femmes, Paris: Gallimard-L'Arpenteur, 1992 / Gallimard-Folio, 1994.
C'est la guerre, Paris: Gallimard-L'Arpenteur, 1993 / Gallimard-Folio, 1996.
L'Homme vivant, Paris: Gallimard-L'Arpenteur, 1994.
Le Monologue, Paris: Gallimard-L'Arpenteur, 1996.
Le Sang violet de l'améthyste, Paris: Gallimard-L'Arpenteur, 1998.
Suite villageoise, Saint-Claude-de-Diray: Éditions Hesse, 2000.
Maître Faust, Paris: Gallimard-L'Arpenteur, 2001.
Les Fontaines silencieuses, Paris: Gallimard-L'Arpenteur, 2005.
K.M. 500, Saint-Benoît-du-Sault: Éditions Tarabuste, 2008.

POETRY
Rag-time, Paris: Denoël, 1972 / Paris: Gallimard-Folio, 1996.
Rag-time (followed by *Londoniennes* and *Poèmes ébouillantés*), Paris: Gallimard-Poésie, 1996.
Paraphe, Paris: Denoël, 1974 / Paris: Arléa, 2011.
Londoniennes, cover by Jacques Truphémus, Paris: Éditions Le Tout sur le Tout, 1985 / Paris: Gallimard-Folio, 1996.
Décalcomanies, lithograph by Pierre Ardouvin, Vercheny: Éditions Grande Nature, 1987.
A.B.C.D., *Enfantines*, illustrated by Jacques Truphémus, Lausanne: Éditions Bellefontaine, 1987.
Nuit close, Paris: Éditions Fourbis, 1988.
Télégrammes de nuit, lithographs by Catherine Seghers, Blois and Saint-Benoît-du-Sault: Éditions La Marge et Tarabuste, 1989.

Danse découpage, illustrated by Philippe Cognée, Saint-Benoît-du-Sault: Éditions Tarabuste, 1989.
Haïkaï du jardin, Paris: Gallimard-L'Arpenteur, 1991
Faire-part, illustrated by the author, Paris: Éditions Deyrolle, 1991.
Silex (in *Rag-time*), illustrated by Jacques Truphémus, Menthon-Saint-Bernard: Éditions Les Sillons du Temps, 1991.
Fruits, illustrated by the author, Saint-Claude-de-Diray: Éditions Hesse, 1992.
Bilboquet, cover by the author, Paris: L'Arbre à Lettres, 1993.
Petit dictionnaire à manivelle, illustrated by the author, Paris: L'Oeil de la Lettre, 1993.
L'Arbre à sanglots, engraving by the author, Ivry-sur-Seine: Atelier d'art Vincent Rougier, 1993.
Les métamorphoses du revolver, illustrated by Franck Na, Saint-Montan: Éditions Vestige, 1993.
Ton nom est sexe, illustrated by Denis Pouppeville, Paris: Éditions Les Autodidactes, 1994.
Nativité, illustrated by Lise-Marie Brochen, Christine Crozat, Claire Lesteven, Frédérique Lucien, Kate van Houten, Marie-Laure Viale, Saint-Benoît-du-Sault: Éditions Tarabuste, 1994.
Bazar narcotique (followed by *États du sommeil I*), Saint-Benoît-du-Sault: Éditions Tarabuste, 1995.
Ouroboros, Saint-Benoît-du-Sault: Éditions Tarabuste, 1995.
Cerf-volant (followed by *Passe-boules*), Saint-Benoît-du-Sault: Éditions Tarabuste, 1995.
Colin-maillard, Saint-Benoît-du-Sault: Éditions Tarabuste, 1995.
Diabolo (followed by *Chat perché*), Saint-Benoît-du-Sault: Éditions Tarabuste, 1995.
Voyage stellaire, Saint-Benoît-du-Sault: Éditions Tarabuste, 1995.
Une allumette prend feu, pisschtt, livre pour enfants-poètes, illustrated by the author, Saint-Benoît-du-Sault: Éditions Tarabuste, 1995.
Non-lieu, Saint-Benoît-du-Sault: Éditions Tarabuste, 1996.
Pile ou face (followed by *Saute-mouton*), Saint-Benoît-du-Sault: Éditions Tarabuste, 1996.
Haute trahison (followed by *Balcon tropical*), Saint-Benoît-du-Sault: Éditions Tarabuste, 1996.
Droguerie du ciel, Saint-Claude-de-Diray: Éditions Hesse, 1996.
Chants d'un autre monde, Saint-Benoît-du-Sault: Éditions Tarabuste, 1996.
Chiffre, Saint-Benoît-du-Sault: Éditions Tarabuste, 1996.
Greffes du temps, Saint-Benoît-du-Sault: Éditions Tarabuste, 1996.
En voiture, s'il vous plaît, livre pour enfants-poètes, illustrated by the author, Saint-Benoît-du-Sault: Éditions Tarabuste, 1996.
Ci-gît (followed by *Onirographie*), Saint-Benoît-du-Sault: Éditions Tarabuste, 1997.
Frontispice (followed by *Labyrinthe*), Saint-Benoît-du-Sault: Éditions Tarabuste, 1997.
Zéro, Saint-Benoît-du-Sault: Éditions Tarabuste, 1997.
Langages, Saint-Benoît-du-Sault: Éditions Tarabuste, 1997.
Je (followed by *Chanson verte*), Saint-Benoît-du-Sault: Éditions Tarabuste, 1997.
Noces funèbres, Saint-Benoît-du-Sault: Éditions Tarabuste, 1997.
Fac-similé, Saint-Benoît-du-Sault: Éditions Tarabuste, 1998.
Images de l'insaisissable (followed by *États du sommeil II*), Saint-Benoît-du-Sault: Éditions Tarabuste, 1998.
Cours des choses (followed by *C'est comme ça*), Saint-Benoît-du-Sault: Éditions Tarabuste, 1998.

Ricroléphant et Cie, livres pour les enfants-poètes, illustrated by the author, Saint-Benoît-du-Sault: Éditions Tarabuste, 1998.

Ouroboros, illustrated by Erik Dietman, Saint-Benoît-du-Sault: Éditions Tarabuste, 1998.

Poèmes d'autrefois, Saint-Benoît-du-Sault: Éditions Tarabuste, 1999.

Terre céleste, Saint-Benoît-du-Sault: Éditions Tarabuste, 1999.

Imagerie, magie, literary collages, Saint-Benoît-du-Sault: Mollat and Éditions Tarabuste, 2000.

Ouroboros, illustrated by Kate van Houten, Saint-Benoît-du-Sault: Éditions Tarabuste, 2001.

Ouroboros, illustrated by Paul-Armand Gette, Saint-Benoît-du-Sault: Éditions Tarabuste, 2001.

Sauf-conduit, Saint-Benoît-du-Sault: Éditions Tarabuste, 2002.

Ouroboros, illustrated by Bernadette Genée and Alain Le Borgne, Saint-Benoît-du-Sault: Éditions Tarabuste, 2004.

Ouroboros, illustrated by Philippe Cognée, Saint-Benoît-du-Sault: Éditions Tarabuste, 2004.

Ouroboros, illustrated by Françoise Quardon, Saint-Benoît-du-Sault: Éditions Tarabuste, 2005.

Ouroboros, illustrated by Jean-Louis Gerbaud, Saint-Benoît-du-Sault: Éditions Tarabuste, 2005.

Ouroboros, illustrated by Ian Tyson, Saint-Benoît-du-Sault: Éditions Tarabuste, 2005.

Ouroboros, illustrated by Carmelo Zagari, Saint-Benoît-du-Sault: Éditions Tarabuste, 2005.

Ouroboros, illustrated by Jean-Luc Parant, Saint-Benoît-du-Sault : Éditions Tarabuste, 2005.

Pasiphaé, Saint-Benoît-du-Sault: Éditions Tarabuste, 2006.

G.: Isthme de mon Amour, illustrated by Djamel Meskache, Saint-Benoît-du-Sault: Éditions Tarabuste, 2012.

ESSAYS

Les sables du temps, Paris: Éditions Le Tout sur le Tout, 1988.

Droit de cité, Paris: Éditions Manya, 1992 / Paris: Gallimard-Folio, 1994.

Perspectives, illustrated by the author, Saint-Claude-de-Diray: Éditions Hesse 1995.

Art-signal, Saint-Claude-de-Diray: Éditions Hesse, 1996.

THEATER

Aux armes, citoyens!, Paris: Denoël, 1986.

THÉÂTRE COMPLET, illustrated by Catherine Seghers, Saint-Claude-de-Diray: Éditions Hesse:

—*Pièces intimistes* (Trafic — Chez les Titch — Les Miettes — Mo — Tu as bien fait de venir, Paul — L'Entonnoir — Les Derniers Devoirs — L'Aquarium), 1993.

—*Pièces baroques I* (Mégaphonie — Les Mandibules — L'Amour des mots — Opéra Bleu — Le Roi Victor), 1994.

—*Pièces baroques II* (La Bataille de Waterloo — Aux armes, citoyens! — Le Serment d'Hippocrate — Une souris grise — Un Riche, trois Pauvres —Les Oiseaux), 1994.

—*Pièces baroques III* (Black-out — Les Veufs — Clap — Le Délinquant), 1996.

Clotilde du Nord, Saint-Claude-de-Diray: Éditions Hesse, 1998.

La Mort du Prince — Créon, Saint-Claude-de-Diray: Éditions Hesse, 1999.

NOTEBOOKS

Le Chemin de Sion, Carnets I, 1956–1967, Paris: Denoël, 1980.
L'Or et le Plomb, Carnets II, 1968–1973, Paris: Denoël, 1981.
Lignes intérieures, Carnets III, 1974–1977, Paris: Denoël, 1985.
Le Spectateur immobile, Carnets IV, 1978–1979, Paris: Gallimard-L'Arpenteur, 1990.
Miroir de Janus, Carnets V, 1980–1981, Paris: Gallimard-L'Arpenteur, 1993.
Rapports, Carnets VI, 1982, Paris: Gallimard-L'Arpenteur, 1996.
Étapes, Carnets VII, 1983, Paris: Gallimard-L'Arpenteur, 1997.
Trajectoires, Carnets VIII, 1984, Paris: Gallimard-L'Arpenteur, 1999.
Écriture, Carnets IX, 1985–1986, Paris: Gallimard-L'Arpenteur, 2001.
Bilan, Carnets X, 1987–1988, Paris: Gallimard-L'Arpenteur, 2003.
Circonstances, Carnets XI, 1989, Paris: Gallimard-L'Arpenteur, 2005.
Traversée, Carnets XII, 1990, Paris: Gallimard-L'Arpenteur, 2006.
Situation, Carnets XIII, 1991, Paris: Gallimard-L'Arpenteur, 2007.
Direction, Carnets XIV, 1992, Paris: Gallimard-L'Arpenteur, 2008.
Dimensions, Carnets XV, 1993, Paris: Gallimard-L'Arpenteur, 2009.
Le Jardin fermé, Carnets XVI, 1994, Paris: Gallimard-L'Arpenteur, 2010.

INTERVIEWS

Une vie, une déflagration (with Patrick Amine), Paris: Denoël, 1985.
L'Aventure intérieure (with Jean-Pierre Pauty), Paris: Julliard, 1994.
Choses dites (with Pierre Drachline), Paris: Le Cherche Midi, 1997.

CORRESPONDENCE

Correspondance 1969–1994 (with Georges Piroué), Saint-Claude-de-Diray: Éditions Hesse, 2001.

FILMS

Louis Calaferte, film by Raphaël Sorin, 1982.
Les Territoires de Louis Calaferte, film by Michel Van Zele, 1988.
Calaferte, la révolte, film by Cécile Philippe, 1992.
Louis Calaferte, du sarcasme à la prière, film by J.-M. Mersh and J.-M. Deconinck, 1993.
Louis Calaferte, un îlot de résistance, film by Jean-Pierre Pauty, 1994.

TRANSLATIONS OF CALAFERTE'S BOOKS INTO ENGLISH

The Way It Works with Women [*La Mécanique des femmes*], translated by Sarah Harrison, Evanston, Illinois: The Marlboro Press / Northwestern University Press, 1998.
C'est la guerre, translated by Austryn Wainhouse, Evanston, Illinois: The Marlboro Press / Northwestern University Press, 1999.
The Inner Adventure: Conversations with Louis Calaferte (with Jean-Pierre Pauty), Evanston, Illinois: Northwestern University Press / Marlboro Press, 2001.

TRANSLATIONS INTO OTHER LANGUAGES

La Mécanique des femmes:

    La Meccanica delle donne, translated into Italian by Giulio Coppi, Milan: ES, 1994.

    La Mecánica de los mujeres, translated into Spanish by Nuria Rodriguez, Lázaro, Mexico: Editorial Joaquin Mortiz, 1995.

    Mecanica Femeilor, translated into Romanian by Bogdan Ghiu, Bucharest: EST, 2005.

Septentrion:

    Drift, translated into Dutch by C.M.L. Kisling, Amsterdam: Uitgeverij De Arbeiderspers, 1997.

    Settentrione, translated into Italian by Francesco Bruni, Vicenza: Neri Pozza Editore, 2006.

Campagnes:

    På Landet, translated into Swedish by Suzanne Ekelöf, Stockholm: Interculture, 1986.

No man's land:

    No man's land, translated into German by Rudolf Wittkopff, Surkamp Verlag, Frankfurt am Main, 1966.

CRITICAL TEXTS AND SPECIAL ISSUES ABOUT CALAFERTE

Georges Piroué, "Louis Calaferte, portrait en paroles," *Repères*, revue romande (Atelier Payot), No. 7, 1983.

Triages, No. 3, 1992.

Louis Calaferte: La Poésie tue les cons (special issue on Calaferte), *Aube Magazine*, No. 53, Summer 1995.

Louis Calaferte: Le Printemps encore une fois (numerous articles and tributes), Lyon: Bibliothèque Municipale de Lyon / Éditions Paroles d'Aube, 1996.

Triages, Supplément 2004 (special issue on Calaferte, with essays by Pascal Boulanger, Gilbert Lascault, John Taylor, and Jean-Claude Watremez), Saint-Benoît-du-Sault: Éditions Tarabuste, 2004.

John Taylor, "From Darkness to Life (Louis Calaferte)," *Paths to Contemporary French Literature*, volume 1, New Brunswick, New Jersey: Transaction Publishers, 2004.

John Taylor, "'Belief, Magic, Miracle': Louis Calaferte as Poet," *Paths to Contemporary French Literature*, volume 2, New Brunswick, New Jersey: Transaction Publishers, 2007.

Louis Calaferte: Un lieu, une mémoire (articles by Gilbert Lascault, Jérôme de Missolz, André Not, Patrick Pelloquet, and John Taylor), No. 0, Saint-Benoît-du-Sault: Éditions Tarabuste, 2012.

LOUIS CALAFERTE (1928–1994) was one of most prolific and controversial French writers of the twentieth century. Consisting of over ninety titles, his published oeuvre includes some forty poetry collections, six volumes of collected plays, an extraordinarily rich series of notebooks, several books of short prose, and much-debated novels such as *Requiem des innocents* (1952), *Septentrion* (1963), or *La Mécanique des femmes* (1992)—the latter published in an English translation at Northwestern University Press as *The Way It Works with Women*. Drafted at the very end of his life and issued posthumously, *Le Sang violet de l'améthyste* (1998) offers an essential key to the unity of this multifarious body of work.

JOHN TAYLOR is the author of the three-volume *Paths to Contemporary French Literature* and *Into the Heart of European Poetry*—all four books published by Transaction. He has also written seven books of stories, short prose, and poetry, the latest of which are *The Apocalypse Tapestries* (Xenos Books), *Now the Summer Came to Pass* (Xenos Books), and *If Night Is Falling* (Bitter Oleander Press). He writes the "Poetry Today" column in the *Antioch Review* and contributes regularly to the *Times Literary Supplement*. For Chelsea Editions, he has recently translated major selections of the poetry and prose poetry of Pierre-Albert Jourdan and Philippe Jaccottet.